C-2945   CAREER EXAMINATION SERIES

This is your
PASSBOOK for...

Sanitary Engineer II

Test Preparation Study Guide
Questions & Answers

COPYRIGHT NOTICE

This book is SOLELY intended for, is sold ONLY to, and its use is RESTRICTED to individual, bona fide applicants or candidates who qualify by virtue of having seriously filed applications for appropriate license, certificate, professional and/or promotional advancement, higher school matriculation, scholarship, or other legitimate requirements of education and/or governmental authorities.

This book is NOT intended for use, class instruction, tutoring, training, duplication, copying, reprinting, excerption, or adaptation, etc., by:

1) Other publishers
2) Proprietors and/or Instructors of "Coaching" and/or Preparatory Courses
3) Personnel and/or Training Divisions of commercial, industrial, and governmental organizations
4) Schools, colleges, or universities and/or their departments and staffs, including teachers and other personnel
5) Testing Agencies or Bureaus
6) Study groups which seek by the purchase of a single volume to copy and/or duplicate and/or adapt this material for use by the group as a whole without having purchased individual volumes for each of the members of the group
7) Et al.

Such persons would be in violation of appropriate Federal and State statutes.

PROVISION OF LICENSING AGREEMENTS – Recognized educational, commercial, industrial, and governmental institutions and organizations, and others legitimately engaged in educational pursuits, including training, testing, and measurement activities, may address request for a licensing agreement to the copyright owners, who will determine whether, and under what conditions, including fees and charges, the materials in this book may be used them. In other words, a licensing facility exists for the legitimate use of the material in this book on other than an individual basis. However, it is asseverated and affirmed here that the material in this book CANNOT be used without the receipt of the express permission of such a licensing agreement from the Publishers. Inquiries re licensing should be addressed to the company, attention rights and permissions department.

All rights reserved, including the right of reproduction in whole or in part, in any form or by any means, electronic or mechanical, including photocopying, recording, or by any information storage and retrieval system, without permission in writing from the Publisher.

Copyright © 2025 by
National Learning Corporation

212 Michael Drive, Syosset, NY 11791
(516) 921-8888 • www.passbooks.com
E-mail: info@passbooks.com

PASSBOOK® SERIES

THE *PASSBOOK® SERIES* has been created to prepare applicants and candidates for the ultimate academic battlefield – the examination room.

At some time in our lives, each and every one of us may be required to take an examination – for validation, matriculation, admission, qualification, registration, certification, or licensure.

Based on the assumption that every applicant or candidate has met the basic formal educational standards, has taken the required number of courses, and read the necessary texts, the *PASSBOOK® SERIES* furnishes the one special preparation which may assure passing with confidence, instead of failing with insecurity. Examination questions – together with answers – are furnished as the basic vehicle for study so that the mysteries of the examination and its compounding difficulties may be eliminated or diminished by a sure method.

This book is meant to help you pass your examination provided that you qualify and are serious in your objective.

The entire field is reviewed through the huge store of content information which is succinctly presented through a provocative and challenging approach – the question-and-answer method.

A climate of success is established by furnishing the correct answers at the end of each test.

You soon learn to recognize types of questions, forms of questions, and patterns of questioning. You may even begin to anticipate expected outcomes.

You perceive that many questions are repeated or adapted so that you can gain acute insights, which may enable you to score many sure points.

You learn how to confront new questions, or types of questions, and to attack them confidently and work out the correct answers.

You note objectives and emphases, and recognize pitfalls and dangers, so that you may make positive educational adjustments.

Moreover, you are kept fully informed in relation to new concepts, methods, practices, and directions in the field.

You discover that you are actually taking the examination all the time: you are preparing for the examination by "taking" an examination, not by reading extraneous and/or supererogatory textbooks.

In short, this PASSBOOK®, used directedly, should be an important factor in helping you to pass your test.

SANITARY ENGINEER II

DUTIES
Performs professional engineering duties in directing and coordinating the activities of subordinate engineers and technical and clerical personnel in administering a comprehensive sanitary engineering program; performs related duties as required.

SUBJECT OF EXAMINATION
Written test designed to test for knowledge, skills, and/or abilities in such areas as:
1. Principles and practices of sanitary engineering as related to facilities and sewage systems;
2. Principles and practices of sanitary engineering as related to water treatment facilities and distribution systems;
3. Principles and practices of drainage and hydraulic engineering;
4. Design, construction, and operation of environmental projects, including contracts, plans, specifications, and estimates;
5. Devices, procedures, and methods used for industrial wastewater pollution control and monitoring;
6. Preparation of written material; and
7. Administration.

HOW TO TAKE A TEST

I. YOU MUST PASS AN EXAMINATION

A. WHAT EVERY CANDIDATE SHOULD KNOW

Examination applicants often ask us for help in preparing for the written test. What can I study in advance? What kinds of questions will be asked? How will the test be given? How will the papers be graded?

As an applicant for a civil service examination, you may be wondering about some of these things. Our purpose here is to suggest effective methods of advance study and to describe civil service examinations.

Your chances for success on this examination can be increased if you know how to prepare. Those "pre-examination jitters" can be reduced if you know what to expect. You can even experience an adventure in good citizenship if you know why civil service exams are given.

B. WHY ARE CIVIL SERVICE EXAMINATIONS GIVEN?

Civil service examinations are important to you in two ways. As a citizen, you want public jobs filled by employees who know how to do their work. As a job seeker, you want a fair chance to compete for that job on an equal footing with other candidates. The best-known means of accomplishing this two-fold goal is the competitive examination.

Exams are widely publicized throughout the nation. They may be administered for jobs in federal, state, city, municipal, town or village governments or agencies.

Any citizen may apply, with some limitations, such as the age or residence of applicants. Your experience and education may be reviewed to see whether you meet the requirements for the particular examination. When these requirements exist, they are reasonable and applied consistently to all applicants. Thus, a competitive examination may cause you some uneasiness now, but it is your privilege and safeguard.

C. HOW ARE CIVIL SERVICE EXAMS DEVELOPED?

Examinations are carefully written by trained technicians who are specialists in the field known as "psychological measurement," in consultation with recognized authorities in the field of work that the test will cover. These experts recommend the subject matter areas or skills to be tested; only those knowledges or skills important to your success on the job are included. The most reliable books and source materials available are used as references. Together, the experts and technicians judge the difficulty level of the questions.

Test technicians know how to phrase questions so that the problem is clearly stated. Their ethics do not permit "trick" or "catch" questions. Questions may have been tried out on sample groups, or subjected to statistical analysis, to determine their usefulness.

Written tests are often used in combination with performance tests, ratings of training and experience, and oral interviews. All of these measures combine to form the best-known means of finding the right person for the right job.

II. HOW TO PASS THE WRITTEN TEST

A. NATURE OF THE EXAMINATION

To prepare intelligently for civil service examinations, you should know how they differ from school examinations you have taken. In school you were assigned certain definite pages to read or subjects to cover. The examination questions were quite detailed and usually emphasized memory. Civil service exams, on the other hand, try to discover your present ability to perform the duties of a position, plus your potentiality to learn these duties. In other words, a civil service exam attempts to predict how successful you will be. Questions cover such a broad area that they cannot be as minute and detailed as school exam questions.

In the public service similar kinds of work, or positions, are grouped together in one "class." This process is known as *position-classification*. All the positions in a class are paid according to the salary range for that class. One class title covers all of these positions, and they are all tested by the same examination.

B. FOUR BASIC STEPS

1) Study the announcement

How, then, can you know what subjects to study? Our best answer is: "Learn as much as possible about the class of positions for which you've applied." The exam will test the knowledge, skills and abilities needed to do the work.

Your most valuable source of information about the position you want is the official exam announcement. This announcement lists the training and experience qualifications. Check these standards and apply only if you come reasonably close to meeting them.

The brief description of the position in the examination announcement offers some clues to the subjects which will be tested. Think about the job itself. Review the duties in your mind. Can you perform them, or are there some in which you are rusty? Fill in the blank spots in your preparation.

Many jurisdictions preview the written test in the exam announcement by including a section called "Knowledge and Abilities Required," "Scope of the Examination," or some similar heading. Here you will find out specifically what fields will be tested.

2) Review your own background

Once you learn in general what the position is all about, and what you need to know to do the work, ask yourself which subjects you already know fairly well and which need improvement. You may wonder whether to concentrate on improving your strong areas or on building some background in your fields of weakness. When the announcement has specified "some knowledge" or "considerable knowledge," or has used adjectives like "beginning principles of..." or "advanced ... methods," you can get a clue as to the number and difficulty of questions to be asked in any given field. More questions, and hence broader coverage, would be included for those subjects which are more important in the work. Now weigh your strengths and weaknesses against the job requirements and prepare accordingly.

3) Determine the level of the position

Another way to tell how intensively you should prepare is to understand the level of the job for which you are applying. Is it the entering level? In other words, is this the position in which beginners in a field of work are hired? Or is it an intermediate or advanced level? Sometimes this is indicated by such words as "Junior" or "Senior" in the class title. Other jurisdictions use Roman numerals to designate the level – Clerk I, Clerk II, for example. The word "Supervisor" sometimes appears in the title. If the level is not indicated by the title, check the description of duties. Will you be working under very close supervision, or will you have responsibility for independent decisions in this work?

4) Choose appropriate study materials

Now that you know the subjects to be examined and the relative amount of each subject to be covered, you can choose suitable study materials. For beginning level jobs, or even advanced ones, if you have a pronounced weakness in some aspect of your training, read a modern, standard textbook in that field. Be sure it is up to date and has general coverage. Such books are normally available at your library, and the librarian will be glad to help you locate one. For entry-level positions, questions of appropriate difficulty are chosen – neither highly advanced questions, nor those too simple. Such questions require careful thought but not advanced training.

If the position for which you are applying is technical or advanced, you will read more advanced, specialized material. If you are already familiar with the basic principles of your field, elementary textbooks would waste your time. Concentrate on advanced textbooks and technical periodicals. Think through the concepts and review difficult problems in your field.

These are all general sources. You can get more ideas on your own initiative, following these leads. For example, training manuals and publications of the government agency which employs workers in your field can be useful, particularly for technical and professional positions. A letter or visit to the government department involved may result in more specific study suggestions, and certainly will provide you with a more definite idea of the exact nature of the position you are seeking.

III. KINDS OF TESTS

Tests are used for purposes other than measuring knowledge and ability to perform specified duties. For some positions, it is equally important to test ability to make adjustments to new situations or to profit from training. In others, basic mental abilities not dependent on information are essential. Questions which test these things may not appear as pertinent to the duties of the position as those which test for knowledge and information. Yet they are often highly important parts of a fair examination. For very general questions, it is almost impossible to help you direct your study efforts. What we can do is to point out some of the more common of these general abilities needed in public service positions and describe some typical questions.

1) General information

Broad, general information has been found useful for predicting job success in some kinds of work. This is tested in a variety of ways, from vocabulary lists to questions about current events. Basic background in some field of work, such as sociology or economics, may be sampled in a group of questions. Often these are principles which have become familiar to most persons through exposure rather than through formal training. It is difficult to advise you how to study for these questions; being alert to the world around you is our best suggestion.

2) Verbal ability

An example of an ability needed in many positions is verbal or language ability. Verbal ability is, in brief, the ability to use and understand words. Vocabulary and grammar tests are typical measures of this ability. Reading comprehension or paragraph interpretation questions are common in many kinds of civil service tests. You are given a paragraph of written material and asked to find its central meaning.

3) Numerical ability

Number skills can be tested by the familiar arithmetic problem, by checking paired lists of numbers to see which are alike and which are different, or by interpreting charts and graphs. In the latter test, a graph may be printed in the test booklet which you are asked to use as the basis for answering questions.

4) Observation

A popular test for law-enforcement positions is the observation test. A picture is shown to you for several minutes, then taken away. Questions about the picture test your ability to observe both details and larger elements.

5) Following directions

In many positions in the public service, the employee must be able to carry out written instructions dependably and accurately. You may be given a chart with several columns, each column listing a variety of information. The questions require you to carry out directions involving the information given in the chart.

6) Skills and aptitudes

Performance tests effectively measure some manual skills and aptitudes. When the skill is one in which you are trained, such as typing or shorthand, you can practice. These tests are often very much like those given in business school or high school courses. For many of the other skills and aptitudes, however, no short-time preparation can be made. Skills and abilities natural to you or that you have developed throughout your lifetime are being tested.

Many of the general questions just described provide all the data needed to answer the questions and ask you to use your reasoning ability to find the answers. Your best preparation for these tests, as well as for tests of facts and ideas, is to be at your physical and mental best. You, no doubt, have your own methods of getting into an exam-taking mood and keeping "in shape." The next section lists some ideas on this subject.

IV. KINDS OF QUESTIONS

Only rarely is the "essay" question, which you answer in narrative form, used in civil service tests. Civil service tests are usually of the short-answer type. Full instructions for answering these questions will be given to you at the examination. But in case this is your first experience with short-answer questions and separate answer sheets, here is what you need to know:

1) Multiple-choice Questions

Most popular of the short-answer questions is the "multiple choice" or "best answer" question. It can be used, for example, to test for factual knowledge, ability to solve problems or judgment in meeting situations found at work.

A multiple-choice question is normally one of three types—
- It can begin with an incomplete statement followed by several possible endings. You are to find the one ending which *best* completes the statement, although some of the others may not be entirely wrong.
- It can also be a complete statement in the form of a question which is answered by choosing one of the statements listed.

- It can be in the form of a problem – again you select the best answer.

Here is an example of a multiple-choice question with a discussion which should give you some clues as to the method for choosing the right answer:

When an employee has a complaint about his assignment, the action which will *best* help him overcome his difficulty is to
- A. discuss his difficulty with his coworkers
- B. take the problem to the head of the organization
- C. take the problem to the person who gave him the assignment
- D. say nothing to anyone about his complaint

In answering this question, you should study each of the choices to find which is best. Consider choice "A" – Certainly an employee may discuss his complaint with fellow employees, but no change or improvement can result, and the complaint remains unresolved. Choice "B" is a poor choice since the head of the organization probably does not know what assignment you have been given, and taking your problem to him is known as "going over the head" of the supervisor. The supervisor, or person who made the assignment, is the person who can clarify it or correct any injustice. Choice "C" is, therefore, correct. To say nothing, as in choice "D," is unwise. Supervisors have and interest in knowing the problems employees are facing, and the employee is seeking a solution to his problem.

2) True/False Questions

The "true/false" or "right/wrong" form of question is sometimes used. Here a complete statement is given. Your job is to decide whether the statement is right or wrong.

SAMPLE: A roaming cell-phone call to a nearby city costs less than a non-roaming call to a distant city.

This statement is wrong, or false, since roaming calls are more expensive.

This is not a complete list of all possible question forms, although most of the others are variations of these common types. You will always get complete directions for answering questions. Be sure you understand *how* to mark your answers – ask questions until you do.

V. RECORDING YOUR ANSWERS

Computer terminals are used more and more today for many different kinds of exams.
For an examination with very few applicants, you may be told to record your answers in the test booklet itself. Separate answer sheets are much more common. If this separate answer sheet is to be scored by machine – and this is often the case – it is highly important that you mark your answers correctly in order to get credit.
An electronic scoring machine is often used in civil service offices because of the speed with which papers can be scored. Machine-scored answer sheets must be marked with a pencil, which will be given to you. This pencil has a high graphite content which responds to the electronic scoring machine. As a matter of fact, stray dots may register as answers, so do not let your pencil rest on the answer sheet while you are pondering the correct answer. Also, if your pencil lead breaks or is otherwise defective, ask for another.

Since the answer sheet will be dropped in a slot in the scoring machine, be careful not to bend the corners or get the paper crumpled.

The answer sheet normally has five vertical columns of numbers, with 30 numbers to a column. These numbers correspond to the question numbers in your test booklet. After each number, going across the page are four or five pairs of dotted lines. These short dotted lines have small letters or numbers above them. The first two pairs may also have a "T" or "F" above the letters. This indicates that the first two pairs only are to be used if the questions are of the true-false type. If the questions are multiple choice, disregard the "T" and "F" and pay attention only to the small letters or numbers.

Answer your questions in the manner of the sample that follows:

32. The largest city in the United States is
    A. Washington, D.C.
    B. New York City
    C. Chicago
    D. Detroit
    E. San Francisco

1) Choose the answer you think is best. (New York City is the largest, so "B" is correct.)
2) Find the row of dotted lines numbered the same as the question you are answering. (Find row number 32)
3) Find the pair of dotted lines corresponding to the answer. (Find the pair of lines under the mark "B.")
4) Make a solid black mark between the dotted lines.

VI. BEFORE THE TEST

Common sense will help you find procedures to follow to get ready for an examination. Too many of us, however, overlook these sensible measures. Indeed, nervousness and fatigue have been found to be the most serious reasons why applicants fail to do their best on civil service tests. Here is a list of reminders:

- Begin your preparation early – Don't wait until the last minute to go scurrying around for books and materials or to find out what the position is all about.
- Prepare continuously – An hour a night for a week is better than an all-night cram session. This has been definitely established. What is more, a night a week for a month will return better dividends than crowding your study into a shorter period of time.
- Locate the place of the exam – You have been sent a notice telling you when and where to report for the examination. If the location is in a different town or otherwise unfamiliar to you, it would be well to inquire the best route and learn something about the building.
- Relax the night before the test – Allow your mind to rest. Do not study at all that night. Plan some mild recreation or diversion; then go to bed early and get a good night's sleep.
- Get up early enough to make a leisurely trip to the place for the test – This way unforeseen events, traffic snarls, unfamiliar buildings, etc. will not upset you.
- Dress comfortably – A written test is not a fashion show. You will be known by number and not by name, so wear something comfortable.

- Leave excess paraphernalia at home – Shopping bags and odd bundles will get in your way. You need bring only the items mentioned in the official notice you received; usually everything you need is provided. Do not bring reference books to the exam. They will only confuse those last minutes and be taken away from you when in the test room.
- Arrive somewhat ahead of time – If because of transportation schedules you must get there very early, bring a newspaper or magazine to take your mind off yourself while waiting.
- Locate the examination room – When you have found the proper room, you will be directed to the seat or part of the room where you will sit. Sometimes you are given a sheet of instructions to read while you are waiting. Do not fill out any forms until you are told to do so; just read them and be prepared.
- Relax and prepare to listen to the instructions
- If you have any physical problem that may keep you from doing your best, be sure to tell the test administrator. If you are sick or in poor health, you really cannot do your best on the exam. You can come back and take the test some other time.

VII. AT THE TEST

The day of the test is here and you have the test booklet in your hand. The temptation to get going is very strong. Caution! There is more to success than knowing the right answers. You must know how to identify your papers and understand variations in the type of short-answer question used in this particular examination. Follow these suggestions for maximum results from your efforts:

1) Cooperate with the monitor

The test administrator has a duty to create a situation in which you can be as much at ease as possible. He will give instructions, tell you when to begin, check to see that you are marking your answer sheet correctly, and so on. He is not there to guard you, although he will see that your competitors do not take unfair advantage. He wants to help you do your best.

2) Listen to all instructions

Don't jump the gun! Wait until you understand all directions. In most civil service tests you get more time than you need to answer the questions. So don't be in a hurry. Read each word of instructions until you clearly understand the meaning. Study the examples, listen to all announcements and follow directions. Ask questions if you do not understand what to do.

3) Identify your papers

Civil service exams are usually identified by number only. You will be assigned a number; you must not put your name on your test papers. Be sure to copy your number correctly. Since more than one exam may be given, copy your exact examination title.

4) Plan your time

Unless you are told that a test is a "speed" or "rate of work" test, speed itself is usually not important. Time enough to answer all the questions will be provided, but this does not mean that you have all day. An overall time limit has been set. Divide the total time (in minutes) by the number of questions to determine the approximate time you have for each question.

5) Do not linger over difficult questions

If you come across a difficult question, mark it with a paper clip (useful to have along) and come back to it when you have been through the booklet. One caution if you do this – be sure to skip a number on your answer sheet as well. Check often to be sure that you have not lost your place and that you are marking in the row numbered the same as the question you are answering.

6) Read the questions

Be sure you know what the question asks! Many capable people are unsuccessful because they failed to *read* the questions correctly.

7) Answer all questions

Unless you have been instructed that a penalty will be deducted for incorrect answers, it is better to guess than to omit a question.

8) Speed tests

It is often better NOT to guess on speed tests. It has been found that on timed tests people are tempted to spend the last few seconds before time is called in marking answers at random – without even reading them – in the hope of picking up a few extra points. To discourage this practice, the instructions may warn you that your score will be "corrected" for guessing. That is, a penalty will be applied. The incorrect answers will be deducted from the correct ones, or some other penalty formula will be used.

9) Review your answers

If you finish before time is called, go back to the questions you guessed or omitted to give them further thought. Review other answers if you have time.

10) Return your test materials

If you are ready to leave before others have finished or time is called, take ALL your materials to the monitor and leave quietly. Never take any test material with you. The monitor can discover whose papers are not complete, and taking a test booklet may be grounds for disqualification.

VIII. EXAMINATION TECHNIQUES

1) Read the general instructions carefully. These are usually printed on the first page of the exam booklet. As a rule, these instructions refer to the timing of the examination; the fact that you should not start work until the signal and must stop work at a signal, etc. If there are any *special* instructions, such as a choice of questions to be answered, make sure that you note this instruction carefully.

2) When you are ready to start work on the examination, that is as soon as the signal has been given, read the instructions to each question booklet, underline any key words or phrases, such as *least, best, outline, describe* and the like. In this way you will tend to answer as requested rather than discover on reviewing your paper that you *listed without describing*, that you selected the *worst* choice rather than the *best* choice, etc.

3) If the examination is of the objective or multiple-choice type – that is, each question will also give a series of possible answers: A, B, C or D, and you are called upon to select the best answer and write the letter next to that answer on your answer paper – it is advisable to start answering each question in turn. There may be anywhere from 50 to 100 such questions in the three or four hours allotted and you can see how much time would be taken if you read through all the questions before beginning to answer any. Furthermore, if you come across a question or group of questions which you know would be difficult to answer, it would undoubtedly affect your handling of all the other questions.

4) If the examination is of the essay type and contains but a few questions, it is a moot point as to whether you should read all the questions before starting to answer any one. Of course, if you are given a choice – say five out of seven and the like – then it is essential to read all the questions so you can eliminate the two that are most difficult. If, however, you are asked to answer all the questions, there may be danger in trying to answer the easiest one first because you may find that you will spend too much time on it. The best technique is to answer the first question, then proceed to the second, etc.

5) Time your answers. Before the exam begins, write down the time it started, then add the time allowed for the examination and write down the time it must be completed, then divide the time available somewhat as follows:
    - If 3-1/2 hours are allowed, that would be 210 minutes. If you have 80 objective-type questions, that would be an average of 2-1/2 minutes per question. Allow yourself no more than 2 minutes per question, or a total of 160 minutes, which will permit about 50 minutes to review.
    - If for the time allotment of 210 minutes there are 7 essay questions to answer, that would average about 30 minutes a question. Give yourself only 25 minutes per question so that you have about 35 minutes to review.

6) The most important instruction is to *read each question* and make sure you know what is wanted. The second most important instruction is to *time yourself properly* so that you answer every question. The third most important instruction is to *answer every question*. Guess if you have to but include something for each question. Remember that you will receive no credit for a blank and will probably receive some credit if you write something in answer to an essay question. If you guess a letter – say "B" for a multiple-choice question – you may have guessed right. If you leave a blank as an answer to a multiple-choice question, the examiners may respect your feelings but it will not add a point to your score. Some exams may penalize you for wrong answers, so in such cases *only*, you may not want to guess unless you have some basis for your answer.

7) Suggestions
    a. Objective-type questions
        1. Examine the question booklet for proper sequence of pages and questions
        2. Read all instructions carefully
        3. Skip any question which seems too difficult; return to it after all other questions have been answered
        4. Apportion your time properly; do not spend too much time on any single question or group of questions

5. Note and underline key words – *all, most, fewest, least, best, worst, same, opposite,* etc.
6. Pay particular attention to negatives
7. Note unusual option, e.g., unduly long, short, complex, different or similar in content to the body of the question
8. Observe the use of "hedging" words – *probably, may, most likely,* etc.
9. Make sure that your answer is put next to the same number as the question
10. Do not second-guess unless you have good reason to believe the second answer is definitely more correct
11. Cross out original answer if you decide another answer is more accurate; do not erase until you are ready to hand your paper in
12. Answer all questions; guess unless instructed otherwise
13. Leave time for review

b. Essay questions
1. Read each question carefully
2. Determine exactly what is wanted. Underline key words or phrases.
3. Decide on outline or paragraph answer
4. Include many different points and elements unless asked to develop any one or two points or elements
5. Show impartiality by giving pros and cons unless directed to select one side only
6. Make and write down any assumptions you find necessary to answer the questions
7. Watch your English, grammar, punctuation and choice of words
8. Time your answers; don't crowd material

8) Answering the essay question

Most essay questions can be answered by framing the specific response around several key words or ideas. Here are a few such key words or ideas:

M's: manpower, materials, methods, money, management
P's: purpose, program, policy, plan, procedure, practice, problems, pitfalls, personnel, public relations

a. Six basic steps in handling problems:
1. Preliminary plan and background development
2. Collect information, data and facts
3. Analyze and interpret information, data and facts
4. Analyze and develop solutions as well as make recommendations
5. Prepare report and sell recommendations
6. Install recommendations and follow up effectiveness

b. Pitfalls to avoid
1. *Taking things for granted* – A statement of the situation does not necessarily imply that each of the elements is necessarily true; for example, a complaint may be invalid and biased so that all that can be taken for granted is that a complaint has been registered

2. *Considering only one side of a situation* – Wherever possible, indicate several alternatives and then point out the reasons you selected the best one
3. *Failing to indicate follow up* – Whenever your answer indicates action on your part, make certain that you will take proper follow-up action to see how successful your recommendations, procedures or actions turn out to be
4. *Taking too long in answering any single question* – Remember to time your answers properly

IX. AFTER THE TEST

Scoring procedures differ in detail among civil service jurisdictions although the general principles are the same. Whether the papers are hand-scored or graded by machine we have described, they are nearly always graded by number. That is, the person who marks the paper knows only the number – never the name – of the applicant. Not until all the papers have been graded will they be matched with names. If other tests, such as training and experience or oral interview ratings have been given, scores will be combined. Different parts of the examination usually have different weights. For example, the written test might count 60 percent of the final grade, and a rating of training and experience 40 percent. In many jurisdictions, veterans will have a certain number of points added to their grades.

After the final grade has been determined, the names are placed in grade order and an eligible list is established. There are various methods for resolving ties between those who get the same final grade – probably the most common is to place first the name of the person whose application was received first. Job offers are made from the eligible list in the order the names appear on it. You will be notified of your grade and your rank as soon as all these computations have been made. This will be done as rapidly as possible.

People who are found to meet the requirements in the announcement are called "eligibles." Their names are put on a list of eligible candidates. An eligible's chances of getting a job depend on how high he stands on this list and how fast agencies are filling jobs from the list.

When a job is to be filled from a list of eligibles, the agency asks for the names of people on the list of eligibles for that job. When the civil service commission receives this request, it sends to the agency the names of the three people highest on this list. Or, if the job to be filled has specialized requirements, the office sends the agency the names of the top three persons who meet these requirements from the general list.

The appointing officer makes a choice from among the three people whose names were sent to him. If the selected person accepts the appointment, the names of the others are put back on the list to be considered for future openings.

That is the rule in hiring from all kinds of eligible lists, whether they are for typist, carpenter, chemist, or something else. For every vacancy, the appointing officer has his choice of any one of the top three eligibles on the list. This explains why the person whose name is on top of the list sometimes does not get an appointment when some of the persons lower on the list do. If the appointing officer chooses the second or third eligible, the No. 1 eligible does not get a job at once, but stays on the list until he is appointed or the list is terminated.

X. HOW TO PASS THE INTERVIEW TEST

The examination for which you applied requires an oral interview test. You have already taken the written test and you are now being called for the interview test – the final part of the formal examination.

You may think that it is not possible to prepare for an interview test and that there are no procedures to follow during an interview. Our purpose is to point out some things you can do in advance that will help you and some good rules to follow and pitfalls to avoid while you are being interviewed.

What is an interview supposed to test?

The written examination is designed to test the technical knowledge and competence of the candidate; the oral is designed to evaluate intangible qualities, not readily measured otherwise, and to establish a list showing the relative fitness of each candidate – as measured against his competitors – for the position sought. Scoring is not on the basis of "right" and "wrong," but on a sliding scale of values ranging from "not passable" to "outstanding." As a matter of fact, it is possible to achieve a relatively low score without a single "incorrect" answer because of evident weakness in the qualities being measured.

Occasionally, an examination may consist entirely of an oral test – either an individual or a group oral. In such cases, information is sought concerning the technical knowledges and abilities of the candidate, since there has been no written examination for this purpose. More commonly, however, an oral test is used to supplement a written examination.

Who conducts interviews?

The composition of oral boards varies among different jurisdictions. In nearly all, a representative of the personnel department serves as chairman. One of the members of the board may be a representative of the department in which the candidate would work. In some cases, "outside experts" are used, and, frequently, a businessman or some other representative of the general public is asked to serve. Labor and management or other special groups may be represented. The aim is to secure the services of experts in the appropriate field.

However the board is composed, it is a good idea (and not at all improper or unethical) to ascertain in advance of the interview who the members are and what groups they represent. When you are introduced to them, you will have some idea of their backgrounds and interests, and at least you will not stutter and stammer over their names.

What should be done before the interview?

While knowledge about the board members is useful and takes some of the surprise element out of the interview, there is other preparation which is more substantive. It *is* possible to prepare for an oral interview – in several ways:

1) Keep a copy of your application and review it carefully before the interview

This may be the only document before the oral board, and the starting point of the interview. Know what education and experience you have listed there, and the sequence and dates of all of it. Sometimes the board will ask you to review the highlights of your experience for them; you should not have to hem and haw doing it.

2) Study the class specification and the examination announcement

Usually, the oral board has one or both of these to guide them. The qualities, characteristics or knowledges required by the position sought are stated in these documents. They offer valuable clues as to the nature of the oral interview. For example, if the job involves supervisory responsibilities, the announcement will usually indicate that knowledge of modern supervisory methods and the qualifications of the candidate as a supervisor will be tested. If so, you can expect such questions, frequently in the form of a hypothetical situation which you are expected to solve. NEVER go into an oral without knowledge of the duties and responsibilities of the job you seek.

3) Think through each qualification required

Try to visualize the kind of questions you would ask if you were a board member. How well could you answer them? Try especially to appraise your own knowledge and background in each area, *measured against the job sought*, and identify any areas in which you are weak. Be critical and realistic – do not flatter yourself.

4) Do some general reading in areas in which you feel you may be weak

For example, if the job involves supervision and your past experience has NOT, some general reading in supervisory methods and practices, particularly in the field of human relations, might be useful. Do NOT study agency procedures or detailed manuals. The oral board will be testing your understanding and capacity, not your memory.

5) Get a good night's sleep and watch your general health and mental attitude

You will want a clear head at the interview. Take care of a cold or any other minor ailment, and of course, no hangovers.

What should be done on the day of the interview?

Now comes the day of the interview itself. Give yourself plenty of time to get there. Plan to arrive somewhat ahead of the scheduled time, particularly if your appointment is in the fore part of the day. If a previous candidate fails to appear, the board might be ready for you a bit early. By early afternoon an oral board is almost invariably behind schedule if there are many candidates, and you may have to wait. Take along a book or magazine to read, or your application to review, but leave any extraneous material in the waiting room when you go in for your interview. In any event, relax and compose yourself.

The matter of dress is important. The board is forming impressions about you – from your experience, your manners, your attitude, and your appearance. Give your personal appearance careful attention. Dress your best, but not your flashiest. Choose conservative, appropriate clothing, and be sure it is immaculate. This is a business interview, and your appearance should indicate that you regard it as such. Besides, being well groomed and properly dressed will help boost your confidence.

Sooner or later, someone will call your name and escort you into the interview room. *This is it.* From here on you are on your own. It is too late for any more preparation. But remember, you asked for this opportunity to prove your fitness, and you are here because your request was granted.

What happens when you go in?

The usual sequence of events will be as follows: The clerk (who is often the board stenographer) will introduce you to the chairman of the oral board, who will introduce you to the other members of the board. Acknowledge the introductions before you sit down. Do not be surprised if you find a microphone facing you or a stenotypist sitting by. Oral interviews are usually recorded in the event of an appeal or other review.

Usually the chairman of the board will open the interview by reviewing the highlights of your education and work experience from your application – primarily for the benefit of the other members of the board, as well as to get the material into the record. Do not interrupt or comment unless there is an error or significant misinterpretation; if that is the case, do not hesitate. But do not quibble about insignificant matters. Also, he will usually ask you some question about your education, experience or your present job – partly to get you to start talking and to establish the interviewing "rapport." He may start the actual questioning, or turn it over to one of the other members. Frequently, each member undertakes the questioning on a particular area, one in which he is perhaps most competent, so you can expect each member to participate in the examination. Because time is limited, you may also expect some rather abrupt switches in the direction the questioning takes, so do not be upset by it. Normally, a board member will not pursue a single line of questioning unless he discovers a particular strength or weakness.

After each member has participated, the chairman will usually ask whether any member has any further questions, then will ask you if you have anything you wish to add. Unless you are expecting this question, it may floor you. Worse, it may start you off on an extended, extemporaneous speech. The board is not usually seeking more information. The question is principally to offer you a last opportunity to present further qualifications or to indicate that you have nothing to add. So, if you feel that a significant qualification or characteristic has been overlooked, it is proper to point it out in a sentence or so. Do not compliment the board on the thoroughness of their examination – they have been sketchy, and you know it. If you wish, merely say, "No thank you, I have nothing further to add." This is a point where you can "talk yourself out" of a good impression or fail to present an important bit of information. Remember, *you close the interview yourself*.

The chairman will then say, "That is all, Mr. _____, thank you." Do not be startled; the interview is over, and quicker than you think. Thank him, gather your belongings and take your leave. Save your sigh of relief for the other side of the door.

How to put your best foot forward

Throughout this entire process, you may feel that the board individually and collectively is trying to pierce your defenses, seek out your hidden weaknesses and embarrass and confuse you. Actually, this is not true. They are obliged to make an appraisal of your qualifications for the job you are seeking, and they want to see you in your best light. Remember, they must interview all candidates and a non-cooperative candidate may become a failure in spite of their best efforts to bring out his qualifications. Here are 15 suggestions that will help you:

1) Be natural – Keep your attitude confident, not cocky

If you are not confident that you can do the job, do not expect the board to be. Do not apologize for your weaknesses, try to bring out your strong points. The board is interested in a positive, not negative, presentation. Cockiness will antagonize any board member and make him wonder if you are covering up a weakness by a false show of strength.

2) Get comfortable, but don't lounge or sprawl

Sit erectly but not stiffly. A careless posture may lead the board to conclude that you are careless in other things, or at least that you are not impressed by the importance of the occasion. Either conclusion is natural, even if incorrect. Do not fuss with your clothing, a pencil or an ashtray. Your hands may occasionally be useful to emphasize a point; do not let them become a point of distraction.

3) Do not wisecrack or make small talk

This is a serious situation, and your attitude should show that you consider it as such. Further, the time of the board is limited – they do not want to waste it, and neither should you.

4) Do not exaggerate your experience or abilities

In the first place, from information in the application or other interviews and sources, the board may know more about you than you think. Secondly, you probably will not get away with it. An experienced board is rather adept at spotting such a situation, so do not take the chance.

5) If you know a board member, do not make a point of it, yet do not hide it

Certainly you are not fooling him, and probably not the other members of the board. Do not try to take advantage of your acquaintanceship – it will probably do you little good.

6) Do not dominate the interview

Let the board do that. They will give you the clues – do not assume that you have to do all the talking. Realize that the board has a number of questions to ask you, and do not try to take up all the interview time by showing off your extensive knowledge of the answer to the first one.

7) Be attentive

You only have 20 minutes or so, and you should keep your attention at its sharpest throughout. When a member is addressing a problem or question to you, give him your undivided attention. Address your reply principally to him, but do not exclude the other board members.

8) Do not interrupt

A board member may be stating a problem for you to analyze. He will ask you a question when the time comes. Let him state the problem, and wait for the question.

9) Make sure you understand the question

Do not try to answer until you are sure what the question is. If it is not clear, restate it in your own words or ask the board member to clarify it for you. However, do not haggle about minor elements.

10) Reply promptly but not hastily

A common entry on oral board rating sheets is "candidate responded readily," or "candidate hesitated in replies." Respond as promptly and quickly as you can, but do not jump to a hasty, ill-considered answer.

11) Do not be peremptory in your answers

A brief answer is proper – but do not fire your answer back. That is a losing game from your point of view. The board member can probably ask questions much faster than you can answer them.

12) Do not try to create the answer you think the board member wants

He is interested in what kind of mind you have and how it works – not in playing games. Furthermore, he can usually spot this practice and will actually grade you down on it.

13) Do not switch sides in your reply merely to agree with a board member

Frequently, a member will take a contrary position merely to draw you out and to see if you are willing and able to defend your point of view. Do not start a debate, yet do not surrender a good position. If a position is worth taking, it is worth defending.

14) Do not be afraid to admit an error in judgment if you are shown to be wrong

The board knows that you are forced to reply without any opportunity for careful consideration. Your answer may be demonstrably wrong. If so, admit it and get on with the interview.

15) Do not dwell at length on your present job

The opening question may relate to your present assignment. Answer the question but do not go into an extended discussion. You are being examined for a *new* job, not your present one. As a matter of fact, try to phrase ALL your answers in terms of the job for which you are being examined.

Basis of Rating

Probably you will forget most of these "do's" and "don'ts" when you walk into the oral interview room. Even remembering them all will not ensure you a passing grade. Perhaps you did not have the qualifications in the first place. But remembering them will help you to put your best foot forward, without treading on the toes of the board members.

Rumor and popular opinion to the contrary notwithstanding, an oral board wants you to make the best appearance possible. They know you are under pressure – but they also want to see how you respond to it as a guide to what your reaction would be under the pressures of the job you seek. They will be influenced by the degree of poise you display, the personal traits you show and the manner in which you respond.

ABOUT THIS BOOK

This book contains tests divided into Examination Sections. Go through each test, answering every question in the margin. We have also attached a sample answer sheet at the back of the book that can be removed and used. At the end of each test look at the answer key and check your answers. On the ones you got wrong, look at the right answer choice and learn. Do not fill in the answers first. Do not memorize the questions and answers, but understand the answer and principles involved. On your test, the questions will likely be different from the samples. Questions are changed and new ones added. If you understand these past questions you should have success with any changes that arise. Tests may consist of several types of questions. We have additional books on each subject should more study be advisable or necessary for you. Finally, the more you study, the better prepared you will be. This book is intended to be the last thing you study before you walk into the examination room. Prior study of relevant texts is also recommended. NLC publishes some of these in our Fundamental Series. Knowledge and good sense are important factors in passing your exam. Good luck also helps. So now study this Passbook, absorb the material contained within and take that knowledge into the examination. Then do your best to pass that exam.

EXAMINATION SECTION

EXAMINATION SECTION
TEST 1

DIRECTIONS: Each question or incomplete statement is followed by several suggested answers or completions. Select the one that BEST answers the question or completes the statement. *PRINT THE LETTER OF THE CORRECT ANSWER IN THE SPACE AT THE RIGHT.*

1. When filling an empty aqueduct, the valve should be opened

    A. slowly to prevent damage to the aqueduct
    B. rapidly to fill the line as soon as possible
    C. slowly to prevent rapid lowering of the reservoir level
    D. rapidly so that there are no air locks

2. The BEST way of detecting the location of a suspected chlorine leak is by placing a _____ near the suspected leak.

    A. rag, which has been dipped in a strong ammonia water,
    B. match
    C. piece of litmus paper
    D. flow meter

3. The term *run-off* refers to the

    A. amount a valve must be turned in order to open it fully
    B. length of time an electric motor continues to turn after the current is shut off
    C. amount of rainfall which flows from the ground surface into the streams and reservoirs
    D. distance the water falls from the intake gate to the turbine

4. Algae in reservoirs may be killed by using

    A. zeolite B. copper sulphate
    C. sodium chloride D. calcium chloride

5. The one of the following types of valves that USUALLY operates without manual control is a(n) _____ valve.

    A. check   B. globe   C. gate   D. angle

6. Rate of flow of water through a water treatment plant is USUALLY referred to in terms of

    A. c.f.s.   B. c.f.m.   C. r.p.m.   D. m.g.d.

7. In order to make it easier to operate a large valve or gate, pressures on both sides of the valve or gate are balanced by

    A. using weights on each side of the valve or gate
    B. opening a smaller by-pass valve
    C. partially shutting down the water in the upstream line
    D. opening the downstream valve very slowly

8. Leaves are removed from the water entering the treatment plant or aqueduct by

    A. skimming   B. coagulating   C. draining   D. screening

9. Odors, due to gases in the water, are removed by 9.____

   A. surging B. sluicing C. aerating D. clarifying

10. Chlorine residual refers to the 10.____

    A. amount of chlorine that must be added to the water
    B. amount of chlorine that remains in the water after a given period
    C. method of adding the chlorine to the water
    D. method of protecting personnel using chlorine from the effects of the chlorine

11. One of the processes that takes place in an Imhoff tank is 11.____

    A. oxidation B. flocculation C. digestion D. coagulation

12. As used in a sewage disposal plant, *effluent* refers to the 12.____

    A. basic treatment process of sewage
    B. time it takes for complete treatment of sewage
    C. type of control the plant uses for treatment
    D. final liquid coming out of the treatment process

13. A grit chamber operates on the basis that 13.____

    A. grit will settle out of slow-moving water
    B. grit will float and can be removed by skimming the surface
    C. increasing the rate of flow of water will leave the grit behind
    D. spraying water into the air will cause the heavier grit to separate from the water

14. The purpose of sedimentation in any sewage treatment process is to 14.____

    A. aerate the sewage
    B. increase the chlorine content of the sewage
    C. remove suspended matter from the sewage
    D. kill the bacteria in the sewage

15. The final treatment for sludge before it is disposed of is 15.____

    A. drying B. adding chlorine
    C. mixing D. washing

16. The amount of sewage applied to a filter bed is GENERALLY controlled by a 16.____

    A. sluice gate B. flow meter
    C. dosing siphon D. regulating valve

17. Methane gas which results from the sewage treatment process is MOST frequently 17.____

    A. vented to the outside air to prevent injury to plant personnel
    B. used as a fuel in the plant
    C. combined with other gases to render it harmless
    D. burned in the open air

18. The filtering material in a *filter bed* at a sewage treat- ment plant is USUALLY 18.____

    A. activated charcoal B. sand
    C. alum D. ammonium chloride

19. Cleaning sewer lines is USUALLY done by the use of a 19.____

    A. catch basin   B. flushometer
    C. sewer rod   D. center line

20. One of the ways of locating a leak in a water line is by using a 20.____

    A. manometer   B. sounding rod
    C. poling board   D. diffusor

21. MOST sewer pipes are made of 21.____

    A. cast iron   B. agricultural tile
    C. brass   D. copper

22. One of the materials generally used in caulking joints in bell and spigot pipe is 22.____

    A. tar   B. litharge   C. red lead   D. oakum

23. Water pipe must be laid at least two feet below the ground surface MAINLY to 23.____

    A. prevent freezing
    B. discourage malicious tampering
    C. reduce the pressure required to make the water flow
    D. eliminate possibility of damage to roads in case of water main break

24. When soldering copper gutters, the flux that is GENERALLY used is 24.____

    A. sal ammoniac   B. resin
    C. killed muriatic acid   D. calcium chloride

25. A good concrete mix for use in the foundations of a small building is 25.____

    A. 1:2:5   B. 5:2:1   C. 2:5:1   D. 1:5:2

26. When painting steel, red lead is used MAINLY as a 26.____

    A. primer coat so final coat will adhere better
    B. primer coat to protect the steel from rusting
    C. finish coat to protect the steel from the action of the sun and water
    D. second coat to bind the primer and finish coats

27. Studs in frame buildings are USUALLY 27.____

    A. 1" x 4"   B. 1" x 6"   C. 2" x 4"   D. 2" x 6"

28. A cement mortar used in brickwork is USUALLY made more workable by adding 28.____

    A. phosphate   B. lime   C. calcium   D. grout

Questions 29-32.

DIRECTIONS: The following four questions numbered 29 to 32, inclusive, are to be answered in accordance with the rules of the department of water supply, gas and electricity.

29. The term *water course* refers to 29.____

    A. aqueducts only
    B. pipe lines only
    C. natural or artificial streams only
    D. all of the above

30. Where a swimming pool discharges upon or into the ground and the water is not treated, the minimum distance between such discharge and a stream MUST be at least _____ feet. 30.____

    A. 50   B. 100   C. 250   D. 450

31. According to the above rules, clothes may 31.____

    A. be washed in a spring, if the spring does not feed directly into a reservoir
    B. be washed in a spring if the place where this is being done is at least one mile from a reservoir
    C. be washed in a spring provided a chlorinated soap is used
    D. not be washed in a spring

32. Industrial wastes may 32.____

    A. be discharged into a stream provided the stream does not feed directly into a reservoir
    B. be discharged into a stream, provided the point of discharge is at least one mile from a reservoir
    C. be discharged into a stream if the wastes are purified in an approved manner
    D. not be discharged into a stream

33. One method of determining the height of the water in a stream feeding into a reservoir is by means of a 33.____

    A. venturi meter   B. flow meter
    C. hook gage   D. strain gage

34. When digging a deep trench, the sides are USUALLY prevented from caving in by using 34.____

    A. shoulders   B. blocking   C. pins   D. sheathing

35. The FIRST precaution a worker should take before entering a sewer manhole is to 35.____

    A. put on hard-toed shoes
    B. put on safety goggles
    C. check that the next manhole upstream is not obstructed
    D. test the air in the manhole

36. Assume that a fuse blows upon connecting a light load to the circuit. You replace it with the same size fuse, and again the fuse blows.
    The BEST thing to do in this case is to 36.____

    A. connect a wire across the fuse so it cannot blow under such a light load
    B. replace the fuse with one having a higher rating
    C. check the wiring of the circuit
    D. place two fuses in series to prevent blowing

37. Of the following material, the one that is BEST for fill as a subgrade for a road is   37.____

    A. sand
    B. silt
    C. clay
    D. a mixture of sand, silt, and clay

38. When dealing with leaking chlorine, it is IMPORTANT to remember that chlorine is   38.____

    A. highly flammable
    B. made safe by spraying water on it
    C. not corrosive
    D. heavier than air

39. Cast iron pipe is MOST frequently cut with a(n)   39.____

    A. hack saw   B. diamond point chisel
    C. burning torch   D. abrasive wheel

40. Water hammer in a pipe line is BEST reduced by installing   40.____

    A. a pressure regulator
    B. an air chamber
    C. smaller pipes and valves
    D. larger pipes and valves

KEY (CORRECT ANSWERS)

1. A	11. C	21. A	31. D
2. A	12. D	22. D	32. D
3. C	13. A	23. A	33. C
4. B	14. C	24. C	34. D
5. A	15. A	25. A	35. D
6. D	16. C	26. B	36. C
7. B	17. B	27. C	37. D
8. D	18. B	28. B	38. D
9. C	19. C	29. D	39. B
10. B	20. B	30. B	40. B

TEST 2

DIRECTIONS: Each question or incomplete statement is followed by several suggested answers or completions. Select the one that BEST answers the question or completes the statement. *PRINT THE LETTER OF THE CORRECT ANSWER IN SPACE AT THE RIGHT.*

1. When used in conjunction with a centrifugal pump, a foot valve

    A. equalizes the pressure on both sides of the pump
    B. regulates the amount of water flowing through the pump
    C. prevents water in the pump from flowing back down the suction line
    D. adjusts the speed of the pump to the amount of water to be pumped

    1._____

2. Grounding an electric motor is

    A. *good* practice because the motor will operate better
    B. *poor* practice because the motor will not operate as well
    C. *good* practice because it protects against shock hazards
    D. *poor* practice because it increases shock hazards

    2._____

3. The one of the following wrenches that should NOT be used to turn a nut is a _____ wrench.

    A. monkey   B. box   C. stillson   D. socket

    3._____

4. A drill is GENERALLY removed from the chuck of a portable electric drill by using a

    A. drift pin   B. wedge
    C. centerpunch   D. key

    4._____

5. The finished surface of a dirt road is MOST frequently maintained with a

    A. blade grader   B. bulldozer
    C. dragline   D. carryall

    5._____

6. Frequent stalling of a truck engine is MOST probably due to a

    A. weak battery   B. low battery water level
    C. leaking oil filter   D. dirty carburetor

    6._____

7. If the reading of the oil pressure gage on a gasoline motor should suddenly drop to zero, the FIRST thing the operator should do is to

    A. check the filter
    B. inspect the oil lines
    C. tighten the oil pan bolts
    D. stop the motor

    7._____

8. A tractor is to be stored for two months. In order to keep it in BEST condition, it should be

    A. drained of all fuel and oil
    B. lubricated every week
    C. started up periodically and run until warm
    D. steam cleaned and all water drained from the radiator

    8._____

9. Trees suffering from transplanting shock are quickly helped by

    9._____

A. deep watering B. foliage feeding
C. root feeding D. vitamin treatments

10. For MOST rapid healing, trees should be pruned during 10.____

   A. November, December, and January
   B. February, March, and April
   C. May, June, and July
   D. August, September, and October

11. The blades of a lawn mower should be set so that the blades 11.____

   A. firmly touch the bed knife
   B. barely touch the bed knife
   C. clear the bed knife by 1/16 inch
   D. clear the bed knife by 1/8 inch

12. The MAIN reason for mulching is to 12.____

   A. fertilize the soil
   B. prevent erosion
   C. protect plants from the cold
   D. kill insects

13. A compost heap would MOST likely include 13.____

   A. lawn clippings B. sand
   C. stumps of trees D. gravel

14. Of the following statements with regard to *seeding,* the one that is CORRECT is: 14.____

   A. Seeds should be sown on a windy day
   B. The ground should be watered heavily after seeding
   C. Seeding should be done primarily on a bright and sunny day
   D. It is not necessary to carefully apportion the amount of seeds sown

15. Organic matter is often added to soil to better condition it for growing plants. 15.____
    Of the following, the item that is NOT organic matter is

   A. lime   B. peat   C. manure   D. leaf mold

16. Of the following, the BEST way to store coniferous seedlings which cannot be planted 16.____
    for a few days is to

   A. unwrap them and put them in a dark, dry location
   B. place them flat on the ground in a sunny location so they can get plenty of light and air
   C. place them in a trench dug in the earth and cover the root ends with soil
   D. make sure the ball is not loosened and keep in a hothouse

17. Transplanting of seedlings is BEST done in early 17.____

   A. spring   B. summer   C. autumn   D. winter

18. After planting privet hedges, they are frequently cut back to within a few inches of the ground.
    This is USUALLY done to

    A. remove dead parts of the hedge
    B. insure dense growth from the ground up
    C. speed up root development
    D. reduce the possibility of insect damage while the hedge is taking root

18.____

19. *Heaving* of pavements in wintertime is USUALLY caused by the

    A. difference of expansion of pavement and subgrade
    B. freezing of water in subgrade
    C. loss of bond between pavement and subgrade
    D. brittleness of pavement

19.____

20. Erosion of side slopes caused by the action of water is GREATEST when the soil is

    A. silt   B. clay   C. hardpan   D. silty-clay

20.____

21. The MAIN reason for making a crown in a road pavement is to

    A. reduce the amount of paving material necessary
    B. make it easier for cars to go around a curve
    C. drain surface water
    D. increase the strength of the pavement where it is most needed

21.____

22. The MAIN reason for paving ditches at the side of a road is to

    A. prevent damage from cars
    B. permit the ditch to carry more water
    C. prevent erosion of the soil in the ditch
    D. block water from getting under the pavement

22.____

23. Assume that vitrified clay tile pipe, with open joints, is being used as the underdrain for a roadway.
    This pipe should be laid

    A. directly on the bottom of the trench
    B. on a bed of clay
    C. on a bed of peat
    D. on a bed of gravel

23.____

24. A macadam road is one in which the base is GENERALLY made of

    A. asphalt   B. broken stone
    C. concrete   D. stabilized soil

24.____

25. To loosen compacted rocky earth road surfaces, the BEST piece of equipment to use is a

    A. disc harrow   B. drag line   C. bulldozer   D. scarifier

25.____

26. Oiling of an earth road is BEST done

    A. in the winter before the snow falls
    B. when you expect much rain

26.____

C. in the spring during dry weather
D. immediately after snow is cleared from the road

27. Cracks in concrete roads are BEST repaired by filling them with

    A. tar B. grout
    C. mineral filler D. sand

28. When repairing patches in old asphalt pavements, the edges of the patch should FIRST be painted with

    A. the same material used for the patch
    B. kerosene
    C. asphalt cement
    D. asphalt binder

29. The sum of 3 1/4, 5 1/8, 2 1/2, and 3 3/8 is

    A. 14   B. 14 1/8   C. 14 1/4   D. 14 3/8

30. Assume that it takes 6 men 8 days to do a particular job.
    If you have only 4 men available to do this job and they all work at the same speed, then the number of days it would take to complete the job would be

    A. 11   B. 12   C. 13   D. 14

31. The city aims to supply *potable* water. As used in this sentence, the word *potable* means MOST NEARLY

    A. clear   B. drinkable   C. fresh   D. adequate

32. Water, after being purified, should not be turbid. As used in this sentence, the word turbid means MOST NEARLY

    A. cloudy   B. warm   C. infected   D. hard

33. The flow of water is *impeded* by the silt in the bottom of the stream.
    As used in this sentence, the word *impeded* means MOST NEARLY

    A. dammed   B. hindered   C. helped   D. dirtied

Questions 34-35.

DIRECTIONS: Questions 34 and 35 are based on the following paragraph.

Repeated burning of the same area should be avoided. Burning should not be done on impervious, shallow, unstable, or highly erodible soils, or on steep slopes - especially in areas subject to heavy rains or rapid snowmelt. When existing vegetation is likely to be killed or seriously weakened by the fire, measures should be taken to assure prompt revegetation of the burned area. Burns should be limited to relatively small proportions of a watershed unit so that the stream channels will be able to carry any increased flows with a minimum of damage.

34. According to the above paragraph, planned burning should be limited to small areas of the watershed because

    A. the fire can be better controlled
    B. existing vegetation will be less likely to be killed
    C. plants will grow quicker in small areas
    D. there will be less likelihood of damaging floods

35. According to the above paragraph, burning usually should be done on soils that

    A. readily absorb moisture
    B. have been burnt before
    C. exist as a thin layer over rock
    D. can be flooded by nearby streams

36. If a foreman does not understand the instructions that are given to him by the district engineer, the BEST thing to do is to

    A. work out the solution to the problem himself
    B. do the job in the way he thinks is best
    C. get one of the other foremen to do the job
    D. ask that the instructions be repeated and clarified

37. The BEST foreman is the one who

    A. can work as fast as the fastest man in the crew
    B. is the most skilled mechanic
    C. can get the most work out of the men
    D. is the strongest man

38. Complimenting a man for good work is

    A. *good* practice since it will give the man an incentive to continue working well
    B. *poor* practice because the other men will become jealous
    C. *good* practice because in the future the foreman will not have to supervise this man
    D. *poor* practice since the man should work well without needing compliments

39. In dealing with his men, it is MOST important that a foreman be

    A. a disciplinarian   B. stern
    C. fair   D. chummy with his men

40. When issuing a violation to a member of the public, it is MOST important that a foreman be

    A. aloof and refuse to discuss the violation
    B. stern, and warn the person to correct the violation immediately
    C. courteous and explain what must be done to correct the violation
    D. friendly and volunteer assistance to correct the violation

KEY (CORRECT ANSWERS)

1. C	11. B	21. C	31. B
2. C	12. C	22. C	32. A
3. C	13. A	23. D	33. B
4. D	14. B	24. B	34. D
5. A	15. A	25. D	35. A
6. D	16. C	26. C	36. D
7. D	17. A	27. A	37. C
8. C	18. B	28. C	38. A
9. B	19. B	29. C	39. C
10. B	20. A	30. B	40. C

EXAMINATION SECTION
TEST 1

DIRECTIONS: Each question or incomplete statement is followed by several suggested answers or completions. Select the one that BEST answers the question or completes the statement. *PRINT THE LETTER OF THE CORRECT ANSWER IN THE SPACE AT THE RIGHT.*

1. If cast iron weighs 450 pounds per cubic foot, the weight of a solid cast iron manhole cover 2 feet in diameter and 1 inch thick is MOST NEARLY _____ pounds.

    A. 94 B. 118 C. 136 D. 164

    1._____

2. A gas which has an odor similar to rotten eggs is

    A. argon
    B. phosgene
    C. nitrogen
    D. hydrogen sulfide

    2._____

3. The gases released by digesting sewage sludges contain about 72%

    A. methane B. chlorine C. helium D. copper

    3._____

4. In sewer maintenance, an orange peel bucket is USUALLY used for

    A. testing for toxic gases
    B. rodding sewers
    C. cleaning roof drains
    D. cleaning catch basins

    4._____

5. A plumbing device that prevents the passage of bad odors and gases from the sewer system to a building is a

    A. corporation stop
    B. union
    C. curb box
    D. trap

    5._____

6. An 8-inch diameter sewer enters at the upstream side of a manhole, and a 10-inch sewer leaves at the downstream side. The crowns of the sewers are at the same elevation. If the invert elevation of the 8-inch sewer is 100.64 feet, the invert elevation of the 10-inch sewer is MOST NEARLY _____ feet.

    A. 100.32 B. 100.41 C. 100.47 D. 100.52

    6._____

7. Where ground slopes are unfavorable, it is necessary to keep sanitary sewer grades at the minimum velocity that will prevent the settling of material when the sewer is flowing full.
    The velocity is MOST NEARLY _____ feet per second.

    A. 0.2 B. 2.0 C. 20.0 D. 200.0

    7._____

8. A condition that will permit polluted water to enter a potable water supply is a

    A. tide gate
    B. cross connection
    C. cathodic protection
    D. reducer

    8._____

9. A wheel with a grooved rim, such as is mounted in a pulley block to guide rope or cable, is a

    A. turnbuckle
    B. wormgear
    C. slant
    D. sheave

    9._____

10. A device used in a combined sewer to bypass excess storm-flow is a(n)

    A. soffit B. side-flow weir
    C. aquafer D. cellular cofferdam

11. A device installed at the discharge end of a sewer outfall which operates to permit gravity flow at low stages in the receiving waters, but closes to prevent backflow when the elevation of the receiving waters is high, is a

    A. flume B. buttress
    C. tide gate D. flocculator

12. A pipe used to carry streamflow under a highway embankment is a

    A. culvert B. lock C. standpipe D. pitot

13. The pipe on the discharge side of a sewage pump is a

    A. tell-tale pipe B. sump pipe
    C. suction pipe D. force main

14. A model 6520 sewer cleaner is rated at 60 GPM at 1000 PSI. As used here, PSI is an abbreviation for

    A. positive surging inflow B. per sewer invert
    C. pounds per square inch D. pounds per sewer inlet

15. In order to increase culvert efficiency and to prevent undermining of the culvert, the entrance to the culvert is FREQUENTLY provided with a

    A. sump pump B. mud valve
    C. head wall D. scroll case

16. A sewer plan calls for pipe diameters of 3", 10", 12", 14", 15", and 18". The size which is NOT used for a standard strength clay sewer pipe is

    A. 10" B. 12" C. 14" D. 15"

17. Lateral sanitary sewers should PREFERABLY intersect at a

    A. catch basin B. weir
    C. manhole D. tide gate

18. A dip, or sag, used in a sewer line to pass under structures, such as subways, is called a(n)

    A. outfall B. inverted siphon
    C. force main D. regulator

19. A device suitable for pumping sewage from deep basements into city sewers is a

    A. pressure relief valve B. vacuum breaker
    C. pneumatic ejector D. comminutor

20. The flow of ground water into sanitary sewers through defective joints is called

    A. back siphonage B. infiltration
    C. overflow D. exfiltration

KEY (CORRECT ANSWERS)

1.	B	11.	C
2.	D	12.	A
3.	A	13.	D
4.	D	14.	C
5.	D	15.	C
6.	C	16.	C
7.	B	17.	C
8.	B	18.	B
9.	D	19.	C
10.	B	20.	B

TEST 2

DIRECTIONS: Each question or incomplete statement is followed by several suggested answers or completions. Select the one that BEST answers the question or completes the statement. *PRINT THE LETTER OF THE CORRECT ANSWER IN THE SPACE AT THE RIGHT.*

1. In a combined sewer system, the amount of sewage flowing to the treatment plant is USUALLY controlled by a   1.____

   A. regulator
   B. bar screen
   C. siphon
   D. mud valve

2. The LOWEST portion of the inside of a sewer pipe is the   2.____

   A. crown
   B. haunch
   C. invert
   D. spring line

3. A.C. pipe, sometimes used instead of clay sewer pipe, is made of   3.____

   A. reinforced concrete
   B. polyvinyl
   C. asbestos and cement
   D. asphalt

4. Of the following, the one which is NOT a sewer cleaning tool is the   4.____

   A. gouge
   B. wire brush
   C. pilaster
   D. claw

5. A sewer rodding machine has speeds up to 100 FPM. As used here, FPM is an abbreviation for feet per   5.____

   A. million   B. mile   C. minute   D. module

6. The nominal diameter of a #4 reinforcing bar is MOST NEARLY   6.____

   A. 0.4"   B. 0.04"   C. 0.5"   D. 4 mm

7. In a 1:2:3 concrete mix, the number 3 represents the proportion of   7.____

   A. sand
   B. water
   C. coarse aggregate
   D. cement

8. Of the following, a procedure used for causing air to flow into and from the lungs of the body by mechanical or manual methods is called   8.____

   A. irrigation
   B. traction
   C. traumatic shock
   D. artificial respiration

9. The one of the following that is a toxic gas which is colorless and odorless is   9.____

   A. chlorine
   B. hydrogen sulfide
   C. carbon monoxide
   D. gasoline

10. In first aid, a tourniquet is MOST often used to   10.____

    A. improve respiration
    B. treat burns
    C. treat sprains
    D. control bleeding

2 (#2)

11. Persons who have been injured may suffer a depressed condition of many of the body functions due to failure of enough blood to circulate through the body. This condition is called   11._____

    A. immunization   B. chronic
    C. cathartic   D. shock

12. The type of injury which is MOST likely to cause lockjaw (tetanus) is   12._____

    A. an epileptic convulsion   B. a puncture wound
    C. an electric shock   D. sunstroke

13. Wellpoints are used in sewer construction PRIMARILY to   13._____

    A. remove gases   B. dewater trenches
    C. locate wells   D. replace hydrants

14. A sewer which carries only sewage from the plumbing fixtures in a house is a   14._____

    A. storm sewer   B. combined sewer
    C. sanitary sewer   D. subsurface drain

15. The slope of a sewer is MOST usually indicated by the units,   15._____

    A. feet   B. rods   C. percent   D. diameters

16. Longitudinal timbers used to support the vertical sheeting in a sewer trench excavation are called   16._____

    A. wales   B. cross braces
    C. piles   D. cradles

17. The sum of 2 5/8, 3 3/16, 1 1/2, and 4 1/4 is   17._____

    A. 9 13/16   B. 10 7/16   C. 11 9/16   D. 13 3/16

Questions 18-20.

DIRECTIONS: Questions 18 through 20 should be answered by selecting the word that MOST NEARLY means the SAME as the word in capital letters.

18. SUPPLEMENT   18._____

    A. terminal   B. absence   C. addition   D. void

19. HAZARDOUS   19._____

    A. dense   B. safe   C. dangerous   D. high

20. VERIFY   20._____

    A. climb   B. travel   C. slide   D. confirm

KEY (CORRECT ANSWERS)

1. A
2. C
3. C
4. C
5. C

6. C
7. C
8. D
9. C
10. D

11. D
12. B
13. B
14. C
15. C

16. A
17. C
18. C
19. C
20. D

EXAMINATION SECTION
TEST 1

DIRECTIONS: Each question or incomplete statement is followed by several suggested answers or completions. Select the one that BEST answers the question or completes the statement. *PRINT THE LETTER OF THE CORRECT ANSWER IN THE SPACE AT THE RIGHT.*

1. A mass diagram is used in water supply computations to determine the
   A. size of the area that will be flooded when a dam is built
   B. capacity of reservoir required to supply the demand for water
   C. volume of excavation required to clear the site for a reservoir
   D. rate of flow of water into a reservoir

2. The velocity head in a pipe is equal to
   A. $\frac{v^2}{2g}$ B. $\frac{v^2}{g}$ C. $\frac{v}{2g}$ D. $\frac{v}{g}$

3. A force of 200 lbs. and a force of 300 lbs. make an angle of 30° with each other. The value of the resultant force is, in lbs., MOST NEARLY
   A. 483   B. 48   C. 493   D. 513

4. A chemical commonly used for coagulation in a water purification plant is
   A. alum   B. caustic ash   C. potash   D. saltpeter

5. The consistency of a concrete mix is measured with a
   A. water meter   B. viscosimeter
   C. slump cone   D. vicat needle

6. The term *4000 pound concrete* commonly means
   A. one cubic yard of concrete weighs approximately 4000 pounds
   B. the allowable stress in compression in the concrete is 400 lb./sq.in.
   C. the concrete has a minimum ultimate strength in compression of 4000 lb./sq.in. at 28 days
   D. the concrete can carry a bond stress of 4000 lb./sq.in.

Questions 7-9.

DIRECTIONS: Questions 7 through 9 refer to the sketch of a reinforced concrete beam.

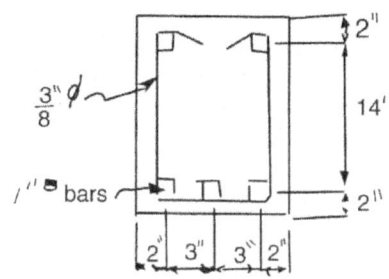

7. The effective width of the beam is, in inches, MOST NEARLY
   A. 5   B. 8   C. 9   D. 10

8. The ³/₈" diameter bar is _____ reinforcement.
   A. temperature
   B. tension
   C. compression
   D. shear

9. Provided no 1" bars are bent up, the upper two square bars are _____ reinforcement.
   A. temperature
   B. tension
   C. compression
   D. shear

10. The sine of 120° is the same as the sine of
    A. 45°
    B. 60°
    C. 45°, but with a negative sign
    D. 60° but with a negative sign

11. The formula for the area of a triangle is
    A. ½ab sin A   B. ½bc sin A   C. ½ac cos A   D. ½ab cos A

12. The logarithm of 7 is approximately 0.845.
    The logarithm of (0.007)¼ is APPROXIMATELY
    A. 9.343-10   B. 9.567-10   C. 9.461-10   D. 9.561-10

13. The center of gravity of a triangle is located at the intersection of the
    A. angle bisectors
    B. medians
    C. perpendicular bisectors of the sides
    D. radians

14. The distance between two stations was measured six times and the average distance found to be 346.215 ft.
    If one measurement of 351.205 ft. is deleted from the data as being inconsistent with the other measurements, then the average of the remaining five measurements is, in ft.,
    A. 345.217   B. 345.221   C. 345.227   D. 345.235

15. A ma of an area 380 ft. x 740 ft. is to be plotted on a sheet of drawing paper. The SMALLEST sheet of paper required to plot this map to a scale of 1" = 50', leaving a one inch margin all around, is, in inches,
    A. 8½ x 11   B. 10 x 17   C. 12 x 17   D. 10 x 15

16. On a topographic map, widely spaced contour lines indicate
    A. a gentle slope
    B. a steep slope
    C. an overhanging cliff
    D. the bank of a stream

17. The scale to which a map is drawn is 1" = 800'.
    Of the following, the MOST common method by which this scale would be indicated on the map is
    A. 1/800
    B. 1" = 9600"
    C. 8.0" = one mile
    D. 1/9600

18. The angle formed between one line and the prolongation of the preceding line in a closed traverse is known as a(n) _____ angle.
    A. split
    B. obtuse
    C. direction
    D. deflection

19. When laying out a horizontal circular curve, the deflection angle for a 100 ft. chord is equal to
    A. one-quarter of the degree of curvature
    B. one-half of the degree of curvature
    C. three-quarters of the degree of curvature
    D. the degree of curvature

20. For a given intersection angle, tables of the functions of a one degree curve show the tangent distance to be 1062.0 ft.
    For the same intersection angle and a curvature of 4°, the tangent distance is, in feet, MOST NEARLY
    A. 265.5
    B. 437.9
    C. 649.3
    D. 1153.4

21. The bending moment diagram for the beam shown in the diagram at the right is
    A. A
    B. B
    C. C
    D. D

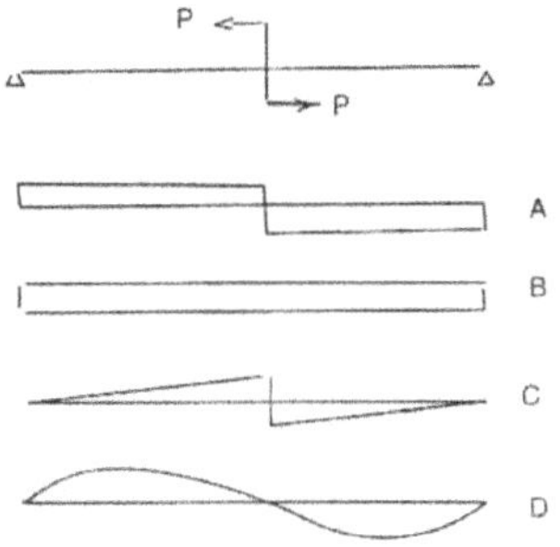

22. The bending moment at the center of a simple beam supporting a uniform load of w pounds per foot throughout its entire length, l, is
    A. $\dfrac{wl^2}{2}$
    B. $\dfrac{wl^2}{4}$
    C. $\dfrac{3wx^2}{8}$
    D. $\dfrac{wl^2}{8}$

23. A simple beam on a 16'0" span carries a concentrated load of 10,000 pounds. If the maximum bending moment in the beam is 465,000 inch pounds, the distance from the load to the nearer support is, in feet, MOST NEARLY
    A. 6.1
    B. 6.3
    C. 6.6
    D. 6.9

24. The section modulus of a rectangular beam 6 inches wide and 12 inches deep is, in inches cubed,
    A. 24
    B. 48
    C. 96
    D. 144

25. A 6" x 8" timber (actual size) is to be used as a beam on a simple span. If the 8-inch side is vertical rather than the 6-inch side, the beam is NOT
    A. stronger in bending
    B. stronger in shear
    C. stiffer
    D. more efficient

    25.____

26. A 6" x 8" timber (actual size) is being used as a gin pole. The radius of gyration of this column which would be used in a column formula to determine safe load for the gin pole is, in inches, MOST NEARLY
    A. 1.73   B. 1.87   C. 1.93   D. 2.13

    26.____

27. A steel rod 25'0" long and 1 inch square in cross-section, fastened to solid supports, is under a tension of 18,000 lb./sq.in.
    If one of the supports yields 0.14 inches, the resultant tension in the bar will be, in pounds per square inch, MOST NEARLY ($E = 30 \times 10^6$ lb./sq.in.)
    A. 3800   B. 4000   C. 4200   D. 4400

    27.____

28. A round steel bar, one inch in diameter and three feet long, is elongated .022 inches by a load applied at one end of the bar.
    The magnitude of the load is, in lbs., MOST NEARLY ($E = 30 \times 10^6$ lb./sq.in.)
    A. 14,200   B. 14,400   C. 14,600   D. 14,940

    28.____

29. A short hollow steel cylinder with a wall thickness of 1.5 inches is to carry a compressive load, applied uniformly on the end, of 1,750,000 lb.
    If the allowable working stress in steel in comparison is 20,000 lb./sq.in., then the minimum outside diameter of the cylinder required to safely support this load is, in inches, MOST NEARLY
    A. 19.4   B. 19.8   C. 20.0   D. 20.2

    29.____

Questions 30-31.

DIRECTIONS: Questions 30 and 31 are to be answered on the basis of the following frame.

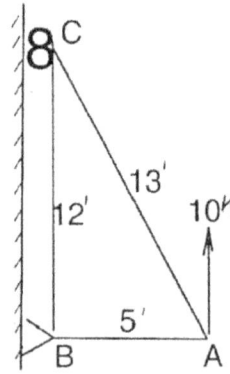

30. The reaction at joint C of the frame is, in kips, MOST NEARLY
    A. 4.17   B. 4.29   C. 4.37   D. 4.63

    30.____

31. The stress in member BC of the frame is, in kips, MOST NEARLY
    A. 10.0   B. 10.6   C. 10.8   D. 11.2

    31.____

32. The modulus of elasticity of aluminum is one-third that of steel. This means that
    A. steel is three times as strong as aluminum
    B. aluminum is lighter than steel
    C. aluminum is three times as strong as steel
    D. for equal stress intensities, the unit strain in aluminum is three times that in steel

32.____

Questions 33-35.

DIRECTIONS: Questions 33 through 35 are to be answered on the basis of the following stress-strain diagram.

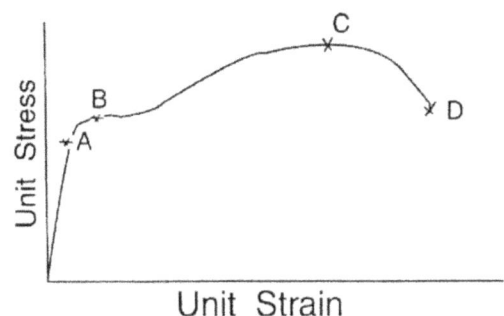

33. The stress-strain diagram is for
    A. high-carbon steel   B. low-carbon steel
    C. cast iron   D. concrete

33.____

34. The yield point is marked
    A. A   B. B   C. C   D. D

34.____

35. The ultimate strength is marked
    A. A   B. B   C. C   D. D

35.____

Questions 36-37.

DIRECTIONS: Questions 36 and 37 are to be answered on the basis of the following sketch.

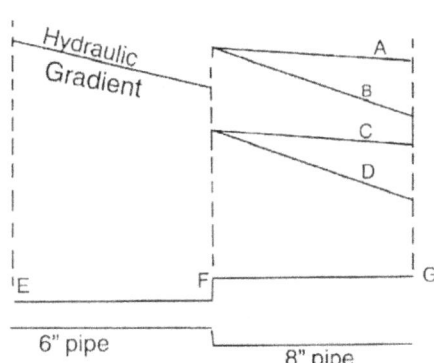

36. The velocity of flow in section EF is 6'/sec.
    The velocity of flow in section FG is, in feet per second, MOST NEARLY
    A. 3.36   B. 3.38   C. 3.40   D. 3.44

37. If the hydraulic gradient as shown from E to F, the hydraulic gradient from F to G is marked
    A. A   B. B   C. C   D. D

38. A 6-inch pipe line is horizontal from point A to point B, the distance AB being 2000 feet. At A, the hydraulic gradient is 10 feet above the pipe; at B it is 2 feet below the pipe.
    The head lost per thousand feet is, in feet,
    A. 1   B. 3   C. 7   D. 6

39. A canal is to have a cross-sectional area of 60 square feet.
    If a square cross-section is used, the hydraulic radius of the canal when flowing full will be, in feet, MOST NEARLY
    A. 2.41   B. 2.45   C. 2.51   D. 2.58

40. If one cubic foot of cement weighs 94 pounds and the specific gravity of the cement particles is 3.10, the void ratio (ratio of volume of voids to volume of solids) is MOST NEARLY
    A. 0.89   B. 0.96   C. 1.03   D. 1.06

KEY (CORRECT ANSWERS)

1. B	11. B	21. C	31. A
2. A	12. C	22. D	32. D
3. A	13. B	23. C	33. B
4. A	14. A	24. D	34. B
5. C	15. B	25. B	35. C
6. C	16. A	26. A	36. B
7. D	17. D	27. B	37. A
8. D	18. D	28. B	38. D
9. C	19. B	29. C	39. D
10. B	20. A	30. A	40. D

SOLUTIONS TO PROBLEMS

3. CORRECT ANSWER: A

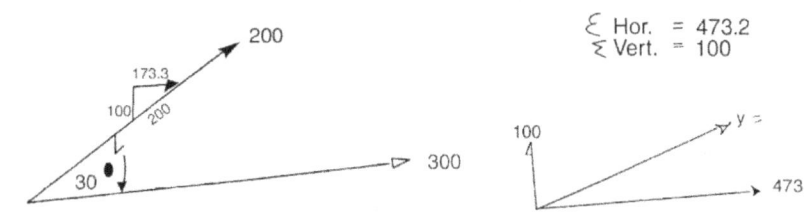

$r = \sqrt{100^2 + 473.2^2} = 483$ lbs.

10. CORRECT ANSWER: B

sin A = sin(π-A); sin 120° = sin 60°

11. CORRECT ANSWER: B

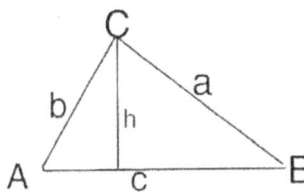

sin A = h/b
Area = $(\frac{1}{2})(c)(h) = \frac{1}{2}bc \sin A$

12. CORRECT ANSWER: C

Log $(0.007)\frac{1}{4} = \frac{1}{4}$log 7 × 10⁻³ = $\frac{1}{4}$(-3+0.845) = 0.539 or 9.461-10

14. CORRECT ANSWER: A

[(6)(346.215) − 351.205]/5 = 1826.085/5 = 365.217

15. CORRECT ANSWER: A
Each dimension on paper must be increased by two inches (one inch margin on each side); 380/50 ~ 8, 740/50 ~ 15 or 10 × 17

19. CORRECT ANSWER: B
Deflection angles for 100 ft. lengths are multiples of ½ degree of curvature.

20. CORRECT ANSWER: A
Since degree of curve is described by the angle subtended by a chord or arc of 100 ft. length, the tangent distance is a direct measure of the degree of curve. For 4°, (1062.0)(¼) = 265.5 ft.

8 (#1)

22. CORRECT ANSWER: D

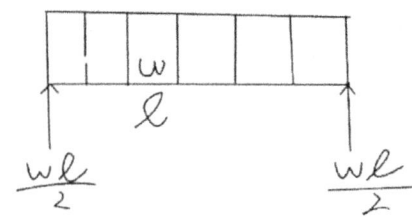

Moment @ $\frac{1}{2} = \frac{wl}{2}\frac{(1)}{(2)} - \frac{wl}{2}\frac{(1)}{(4)}$

from the rt.

$= \frac{wl^2}{4} - \frac{wl^2}{8}$

$= \frac{wl^2}{8}$

23. CORRECT ANSWER: C

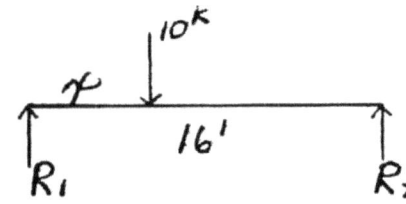

$M = \frac{465000}{12} = 38.750$ ft.-k

$R_1 = \frac{(16-x)}{(16)} 10$

$38.75 = R_1 x = \frac{(16-x)}{(16)}(10)(x) = \frac{160x - 10x^2}{16}$

$10x^2 - 160x + 38.75(16) = 0$

$x^2 - 16x + 62 = 0$

$x = \frac{-b \pm \sqrt{b^2 - 4ac}}{2a}$

$x = \frac{16 \pm \sqrt{256 - 248}}{2} = \frac{16 \pm \sqrt{8}}{2}$

$x = 8 \pm \sqrt{2}$

It must be less than 8 to be the distance to the nearer support ∴ 8 − 1.4 = 6.6

24. CORRECT ANSWER: D

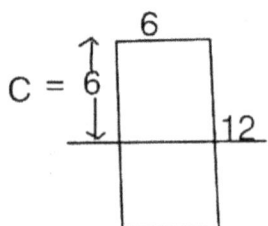

Section Modulus $= \frac{1}{c}$

$I = \frac{bh^3}{12} = \frac{6 \times 12^3}{12} = 6 \times 12^2$

$c = 6$

$\frac{1}{c} = \frac{6 \times 12^2}{6}$ $12^2 = 144$

9 (#1)

25. CORRECT ANSWER: B
By having the 8-inch side vertical rather than the 6-inch side, it becomes stronger in bending, stiffer and more efficient, but the shear strength remains the same.

26. CORRECT ANSWER: A

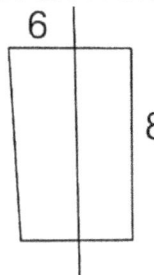

(taken about the weak axis)

$r = \dfrac{d}{\sqrt{12}}$

$d = 6$

$r = \dfrac{6}{\sqrt{12}}$ 1.73

27. CORRECT ANSWER: B
$E = 30 \times 10^6$
$A = \pi/4$
$\varepsilon = \dfrac{\sigma}{E} = \dfrac{18000}{30 \times 10^6} = 600 \times 10^{-6}$

Support yield = 0.14 inches = $\dfrac{0.14}{25 \times 12}$ = 467×10^{-6}

$(600-467) \times 10^{-6} = 133$ in/in

$\sigma = E\varepsilon = 30 \times 10^6 \times 133 \times 10^{-6} = 3990$ psi

28. CORRECT ANSWER: B
$E = 30 \times 10^6$ psi

$A = \dfrac{\pi D^2}{4} = \pi/4$ in²

$\varepsilon = .022/36 = 611 \times 10^{-6}$ in/in

$\sigma = \dfrac{P}{A} = P/\pi/4$

$E = \dfrac{\sigma}{\varepsilon}$

p = $E\varepsilon \pi/4 = 30 \times 10^6 \times 611 \times 10^6 \times \pi/4 = 14{,}400$ lbs.

10 (#1)

29. CORRECT ANSWER: C

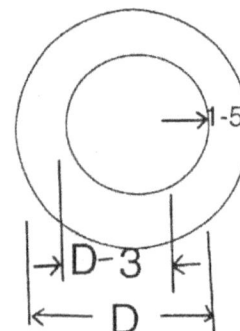

$$A = \frac{P}{\sigma} = \frac{1,750,000 \text{ lbs.}}{20,000 \text{ psi}} = 87.5 \text{ in}^2$$

$$\frac{\pi D^2}{4} - \frac{\pi(D-3)^2}{4} = 87.5$$

$$D^2 - (D^2 - 6D + 9) = 8.75(4/\pi)$$

$$6D = 111.4 + 9$$
$$D = 20.07$$

30. CORRECT ANSWER: A
Horizontal reaction C from ∑M about B =
C(12) = 10 × 5
C→ = 4.17

31. CORRECT ANSWER: A
∑V = 0; BC takes only the vertical loading because of the roller at B.

32. CORRECT ANSWER: D
$E = \frac{\sigma}{\varepsilon}$

Steel E ≈ 30
AlE ≈ 10

$\varepsilon\text{steel} = \frac{\sigma\text{const}}{30} = 1/30$

$\varepsilon\text{al} = \frac{\sigma\text{const}}{10} = 1/10$

$\frac{1 \text{ al}}{10} = 3(\frac{1\text{st}}{30})$

33. CORRECT ANSWER: B
Low carbon steel because of the ductility

36. CORRECT ANSWER: B
Q = flow (ft 3/sec.)   Q = Av
A = area(ft²)   Av = A'v
v = velocity (ft/sec)   (9π)(6) = (16π)v
                              v = 3.38

37. CORRECT ANSWER: A
The hydraulic gradient is a line drawn through a series of points to which water would rise in piezometer tubes attached to a pipe through which water flows. The head loss in the larger pipe due to friction will be at a lesser rate than the smaller pipe because of the larger diameter and lower velocity of flow.

39. CORRECT ANSWER: D

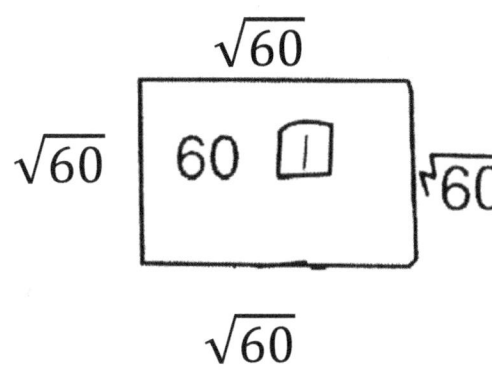

hydraulic radius = $\dfrac{\text{cross-section area of water}}{\text{wetted perimeter}}$

$= \dfrac{60}{3\sqrt{60}} = 2.58$

40. CORRECT ANSWER: D
If there were no voids, the weight of one cubic ft. would be 3.10 × 62.4 = 193.44

Volume of voids = $\dfrac{193.44 - 94}{193.44}$ ft³ = $\dfrac{99.44}{193.44}$

Volume of solids = $\dfrac{94}{193.44}$ ft³

Void ratio = $\dfrac{99.44}{94.00}$ = 1.06

TEST 2

DIRECTIONS: Each question or incomplete statement is followed by several suggested answers or completions. Select the one that BEST answers the question or completes the statement. *PRINT THE LETTER OF THE CORRECT ANSWER IN THE SPACE AT THE RIGHT.*

1. A *plane table* is MOST commonly used to
   A. determine trigonometric functions of angles
   B. plot large maps in the office from data taken in the field
   C. plot maps directly in the field
   D. adjust distances from slope measurements to horizontal measurements

2. Of the following formulas used in taping, the one that gives the correction for sag is
   A. $\dfrac{h^2}{2s}$
   B. $\dfrac{0.204W\sqrt{AE}}{\sqrt{P_n-P_o}}$
   C. $\dfrac{(P-P_o)l}{AE}$
   D. $\dfrac{W^2L}{24P^2}$

3. Recorded distances will be less than the actual horizontal distances when measurements are taken
   A. with the tape on a slope
   B. at a temperature lower than that at which the tape was standardized
   C. with the center of the tape out of line
   D. with a tension greater than that at which the tape was standardized

4. A 100 ft. steel tape is standardized fully supported under a 10 pound pull when the temperature is 59°F and found to be 100.17 feet long. A distance of 70.00 feet is to be laid out with this tape under the standardization conditions.
   The tape distance to lay out, in feet, is
   A. 69.88   B. 69.99   C. 70.01   D. 70.12

5. In the closed traverse ABC, the bearings of lines AB and BC are N45°-00'E and N60°00'E, respectively. The lengths of these lines are 200 ft. and 300 ft., respectively. The bearing of line CA is MOST NEARLY
   A. S54°-00'W   B. S56°-00'W   C. S58°-00'W   D. S60°-00'W

6. A transit is so designed that the stadia constant C is negligible. The stadia interval factor is 200. When the telescope if level,
   A. readings must be taken on the stadia red every 100 ft.
   B. the distance from the instrument to the rod is 100 times the difference between the readings of the upper and lower crosshairs on the rod
   C. the scale used to read the stadia rod is divided into 100 parts
   D. the difference of elevation from the instrument to the point on which the rod is held is equal to the stadia reading plus 1.00 ft.

Questions 7-11.

DIRECTIONS: In Questions 7 through 11, the plan and front elevation of an object are shown on the left, and on the right are shown four figures, one of which, and only one, represents the right side elevation. Indicate the letter which represents the right side elevation.

SAMPLE QUESTION: In the sample shown below, which figure correctly represents the right side elevation?

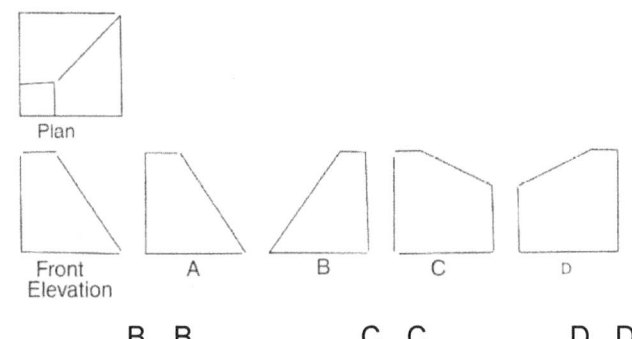

A. A   B. B   C. C   D. D

The correct answer is A.

7.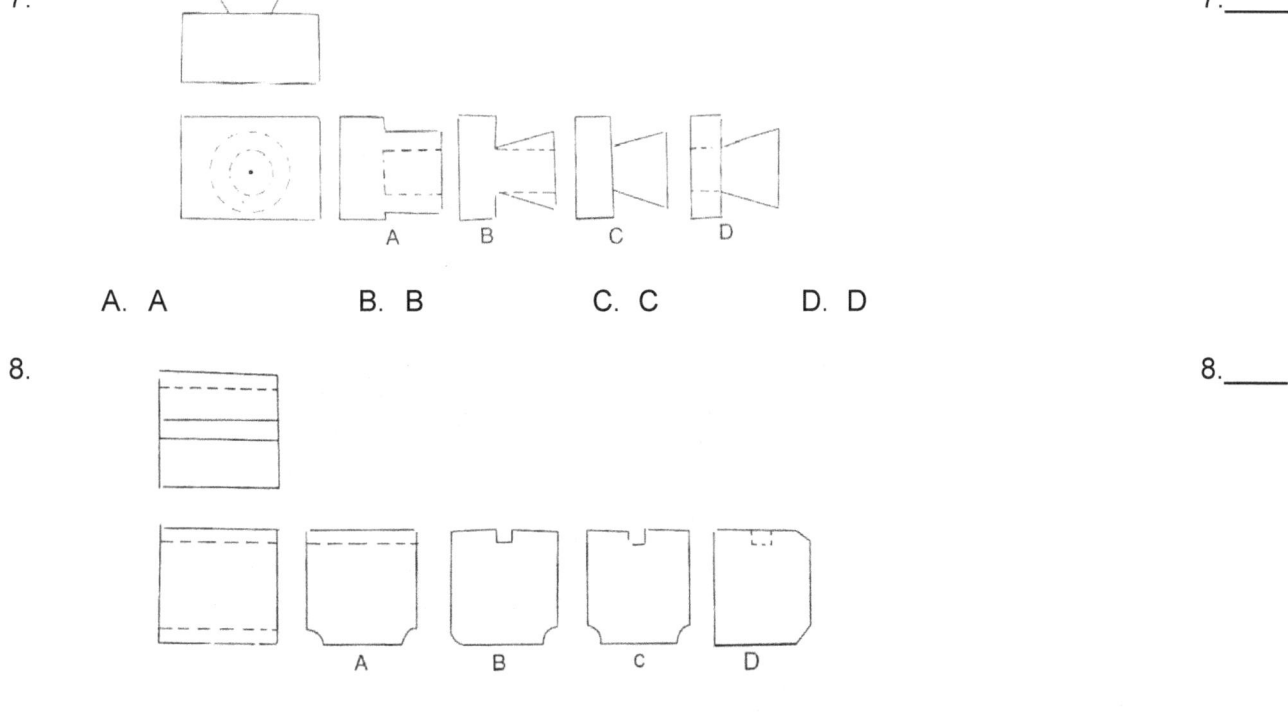

A. A   B. B   C. C   D. D

8.

A. A   B. B   C. C   D. D

9.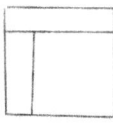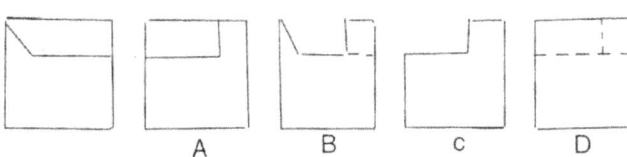

A. A   B. B   C. C   D. D

10.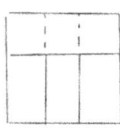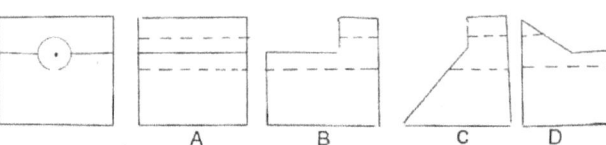

A. A   B. B   C. C   D. D

11.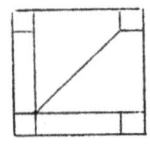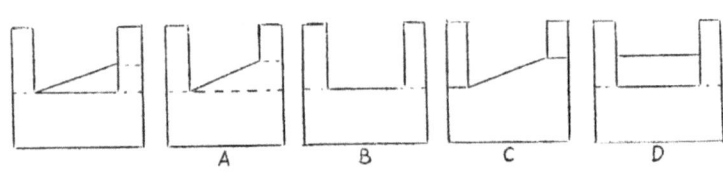

A. A   B. B   C. C   D. D

Questions 12-14.

DIRECTIONS: Questions 12 through 14 are to be answered on the basis of the following sketch.

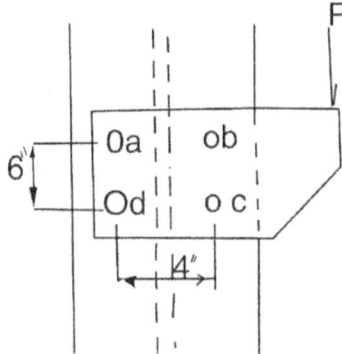

12. Maximum rivet stress occurs in rivet 12.____
    A. a only   B. b only   C. c only   D. b and c

13. The plate carrying the load is known as a _____ plate. 13.____
    A. gusset   B. flange   C. web   D. shear

14. The plate carrying the load is attached to a(n) _____ column. 14.____
    A. built-up   B. H
    C. channel   D. none of the above

15. A 3 x 3 x ³/₈ angle in a structural frame is in tension. It is connected at each 15.____
    end by one ⁷/₈" rivet to a gusset plate.
    The net section of the angle is equal to the gross minus _____ square inches.
    A. 0.339   B. 0.347   C. 0.375   D. 0.389

16. A formula commonly used to determine the allowable unit stresses in columns 16.____
    is s =
    A. $\dfrac{\pi^2 EI}{4l^2}$
    B. $17000 - .485(\dfrac{1}{r})^2$
    C. $\dfrac{22500}{1+\dfrac{l^2}{1800r^2}}$
    D. $\dfrac{P+Mc}{A \pm I}$

17. A rectangular footing 6'0" long by 4'0" wide carries a vertical load of 20,000 17.____
    pounds located on the long axis 5 inches from the center of the footing.
    The maximum soil pressure under the footing due to this load is, in pounds per
    square inch, MOST NEARLY
    A. 1250   B. 1350   C. 1450   D. 1550

18. *Special anchorage* in concrete work commonly refers to 18.____
    A. reinforcement in concrete bolted to steel girders
    B. wing walls on a retaining wall to provide extra support
    C. a hook at the end of a reinforcing rod in continuous beam construction
    D. additional steel dowels connecting a concrete column with a concrete
       footing

Questions 19-20.

DIRECTIONS: Questions 19 and 20 are to be answered on the basis of the following sketch.

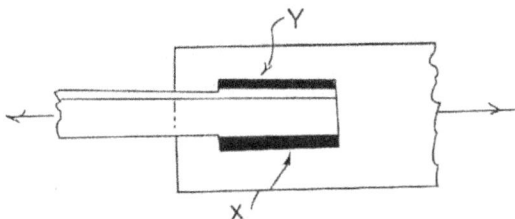

19. In the welded section shown, the length of weld x should be _____ that of y.   19._____
    A. equal to   B. greater than
    C. less than   D. independent of

20. The welds shown are _____ welds.   20._____
    A. single V   B. double V   C. plug   D. fillet

21. The slope at any point on the bending moment diagram for a beam is equal   21._____
    to the _____ the beam at that point.
    A. load on   B. shear on
    C. deflection of   D. slope of

22. The shear diagram for the beam shown in the   22._____
    diagram at the right is
    A. A
    B. B
    C. C
    D. D

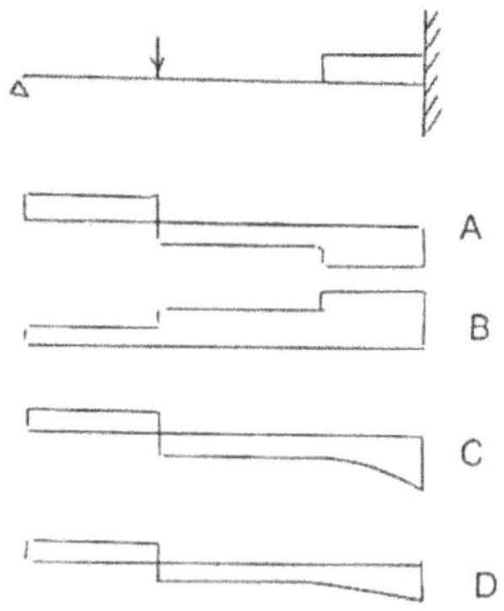

23. Vertical curves in highway work are usually parts of   23._____
    A. circles   B. ellipses   C. hyperbolas   D. parabolas

24. In laying out an angle with a transit, an error of one minute will result in   24._____
    locating a point 1000 ft. from the transit off the true line by APPROXIMATELY
    _____ ft.
    A. 0.1   B. 0.2   C. 0.3   D. 0.5

25. The sum of the positive departures of a closed traverse exceeds that of the   25._____
    negative departures by 0.31 ft. The sum of the negative latitudes exceeds that
    of the positive latitudes by 0.67 ft.
    The linear error of closure is, in feet, MOST NEARLY
    A. 0.39   B. 0.47   C. 0.58   D. 0.74

26. The balanced latitudes and departures of the sides of a closed traverse are   26._____
    as follows:

Line	Lat.	Dep.
AB	+152.27	+212.06
BC	+316.19	+ 83.92
CD	-522.34	+119.30
DA	+ 53.88	-415.28

    The DMD of line CD referred to a meridian through A is
    A. 567.89   B. 635.46   C. 711.26   D. 819.77

Questions 27-31.

DIRECTIONS: Questions 27 through 31 are to be answered on the basis of the following closed traverse which is drawn to scale.

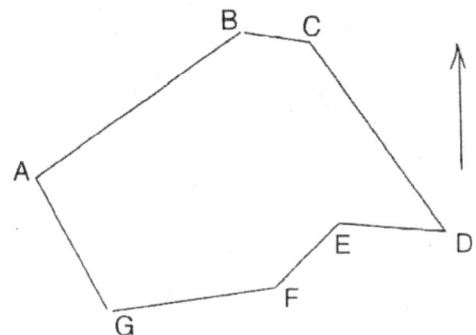

27. The sum of the interior angles of the traverse is
    A. 760°   B. 844°   C. 900°   D. 920°

28. The arithmetical sum of the deflection angles, i.e., the sum without regard to sign, is
    A. 160°
    B. 240°
    C. 330°
    D. greater than 360°

29. When balancing a survey of a closed traverse, the functions of angles most commonly used are
    A. sin and tan   B. cos and tan   C. sin and cos   D. tan and cot

30. Of the following lines, the one with the LARGEST departure is
    A. AB   B. CD   C. AG   D. GF

31. The area of the traverse could not be computed if all sides and angles were measured EXCEPT
    A. angles A, B, and C
    B. sides AB and CD and angle B
    C. side AB and angles A and B
    D. sides AB, BC, and CD

32. The notes for a level run are as follows:

Sta.	BS	HI	FS	Elev.
BM1	3.26			100.23
A	2.13		1.19	
B	4.05		3.20	
C	2.26		4.03	
BM2			4.22	

    The elevation of BMS is
    A. 99.17   B. 99.21   C. 99.25   D. 99.29

33. The foot of a leveling rod has been worn through hard use so that the rod is now .02 ft. short.
    The elevation of any point found, using this rod, will be
    A. .02 ft. low   B. correct   C. .02 ft. high   D. .04 ft. high

    33._____

34. The correction to be applied to high rod readings on a Philadelphia rod is -0.004. In running a level circuit with this rod,
    A. 0.004 should be subtracted from all high rod readings before entering them
    B. the error should be ignored as it will cancel itself
    C. the error should be ignored until all elevations are computed and then corrections should be made to elevations as required
    D. the total error will be 0.004 times the square root of the number of high rod readings

    34._____

Questions 35-40.

DIRECTIONS: Questions 35 through 40 are to be answered on the basis of the following sketch of a transit.

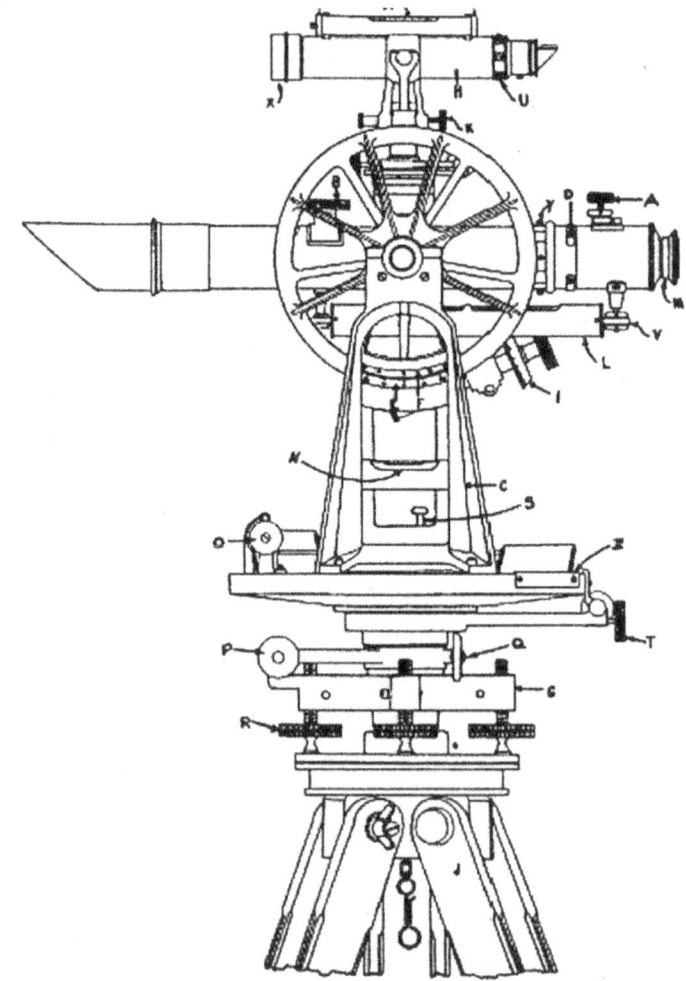

8 (#2)

35. The vertical circle is marked 35._____
    A. D   B. E   C. F   D. I

36. A prism would be attached at 36._____
    A. M   B. U   C. X   D. Z

37. The lower motion clamp is marked 37._____
    A. K   B. P   C. Q   D. T

38. The bubble which would normally be centered to make the line of sight truly 38._____
    horizontal is marked
    A. L   B. N   C. O   D. W

39. The needle lifting or needle release screw is marked 39._____
    A. D   B. K   C. R   D. S

40. A peg test for this transit has been performed, and the line of sight reads 40._____
    4.085 on the far rod. The far rod reading is computed to be 4.060. In making
    the adjustment, the first thing to move is the
    A. bubble adjusting screws
    B. capstan-headed screws on the reticule
    C. vertical slow motion
    D. vertical Vernier adjusting screws

KEY (CORRECT ANSWERS)

1. C	11. A	21. B	31. D
2. D	12. D	22. D	32. D
3. D	13. A	23. D	33. B
4. A	14. B	24. C	34. C
5. A	15. C	25. D	35. C
6. B	16. B	26. C	36. A
7. C	17. A	27. C	37. C
8. B	18. C	28. D	38. A
9. A	19. C	29. C	39. D
10. B	20. D	30. A	40. C

SOLUTIONS TO PROBLEMS

3. **CORRECT ANSWER: D**
   The tapes' lengths are based on a standardized tension. If extra tension is applied, a short reading will result.

4. **CORRECT ANSWER: A**
   The correction to be applied is:
   70/100 × .17 = 0.12
   ∴ 70.00 − 0.12 = 69.88

5. **CORRECT ANSWER: A**
   200 ft. @ N45°E = 2 × 45 = 90°
   300 ft. @ N60°E = $\frac{3}{5}$ × 60 = $\frac{180°}{270°}$

   AC = $\frac{270°}{5}$ = N54°E
   CA = S54°W

6. **CORRECT ANSWER: B**
   This is the definition of the stadia interval factor.

12. **CORRECT ANSWER: D**
    The rivet stress is derived from the vertical load and the moment derived thereof. In this case, the vertical load is equal and the stresses due to moment are equal and additive to the vertical load. The moment stress is subtractive from the stresses on a and d.

15. **CORRECT ANSWER: C**
    The net section = the gross minus the area taken by the rivet 1/8" larger than the rivet used.

    The area subtracted = (8/8+1/8) × 3/8 = 0.375 in².

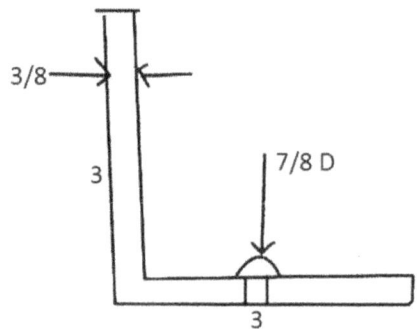

17. **CORRECT ANSWER: A**
    Max. stress = P/A + $\frac{MC}{I}$ C = 3
    I = bh³/12

    = $\frac{20}{6 \times 4}$ + $\frac{(20 \times \frac{1}{2})(3)}{\frac{4 \times 6^3}{12}}$

    = $\frac{20}{24}$ + $\frac{15}{36}$ = .83 + .42 = 1.25K psf = 1250 psf

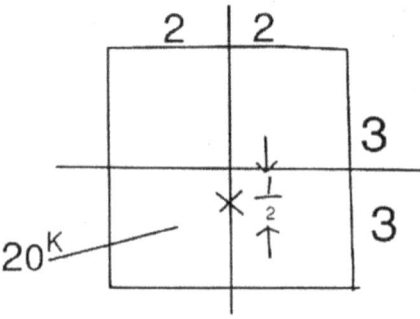

23. **CORRECT ANSWER: D**
Parabolic arc is ideally suited for changes in vertical grade since slope varies at constant rate with respect to horizontal distance.

24. **CORRECT ANSWER: C**
tan 1 minute = 0.00029

α = 1 minute
b = 1000 ft.
$\frac{a}{b} = \tan\alpha$

a = tanα × b = .00029 × 1000 ft. = 0.29 ft.

25. **CORRECT ANSWER: D**

Linear error of closure $= \sqrt{(\Sigma\text{Lat})^2 + (\Sigma\text{Dep})^2}$

$= \sqrt{(0.31)^2 + (.67)^2}$

$= \sqrt{5450}$

= 0.74 ft.

26. **CORRECT ANSWER: C**
AB DMD = 212.06
BC DMD = 212.06 + 212.06 + 83.92 = 508.04
CD DMD = 508.04 + 83.92 + 119.30 = 711.26

The DMD of the first line equals the departure of the first line. The DMD of any other line is equal to the DMD of the preceding line plus the departure of the preceding line, plus the departure of the line itself.

27. **CORRECT ANSWER: C**
(n-2) × 180° = sum of the interior angles
n = number of sides
(7-2) × 180 = 900°

31. **CORRECT ANSWER: D**
There is no way to determine the lengths of these sides. All other missing data could be computed by trigonometry and geometry.

32. CORRECT ANSWER: D
The complete notes should read as follows:

Sta.	BS	HI	FS	Elev.
BM1	3.26	103.49		100.23
A	2.13	104.43	1.19	102.30
B	4.05	105.28	3.20	101.23
C	2.26	103.51	4.03	101.25
BM2			4.22	99.29

33. CORRECT ANSWER: B
Elevations are determined by differences of rod readings; therefore, a short rod does not affect the final data.

TEST 3

DIRECTIONS: Each question or incomplete statement is followed by several suggested answers or completions. Select the one that BEST answers the question or completes the statement. *PRINT THE LETTER OF THE CORRECT ANSWER IN THE SPACE AT THE RIGHT.*

1. A wooden beam is a rectangle 6" x 12".
   On a simple span, the ratio of the uniform load it can carry with the 6" sides vertical to that with the 12" sides vertical is as one is to
   A. 2 B. 5 C. 7 D. 9

2. A moving load consists of a 4-kip and an 8-kip concentrated load spaced 8 feet apart.
   The maximum bending moment caused by this moving load on a simple span of 16 feet is, in kip-feet,
   A. 33.3 B. 31.9 C. 27.6 D. 23.9

3. A canal with a trapezoidal cross-section is 6'0" wide at the bottom and has side slopes of one on one.
   When the depth of water is 4'6", the hydraulic radius is
   A. 2.43 B. 2.52 C. 2.55 D. 2.67

4. The minimum amount of cover required for water mains in city streets is NOT affected by
   A. depth of frost
   B. consideration of shock loads
   C. depth of rock
   D. any of the above

5. A vertical steel tank, 10'0" diameter, wall thickness ¼", is subjected to a hydrostatic pressure of 100 feet of water. The maximum tensile stress in the tank, in lb./sq.in., is MOST NEARLY
   A. 10,200 B. 10,400 C. 10,600 D. 10,800

6. Three eye bars, 6" x 1" x 25'0", jointly, are to carry a load of 200,000 lbs. The middle bar is .03 inch too short. Assuming the pins through the eyes to be parallel, the cross-section of the bars to be uniform throughout their entire length, and $E = 30 \times 10^6$ #/sq.in., the stress in the outer bars in lb./sq.in. will be MOST NEARLY
   A. 10,100 B. 10,300 C. 10,500 D. 10,800

7. A property of steel NOT usually determined in the ordinary commercial tensile test of steel is
   A. modulus of rupture
   B. percent reduction in area
   C. yield point
   D. ultimate stress

8. In the activated sludge process, *seeding* is carried on in the
   A. grit chamber
   B. aeration tank
   C. sand filter
   D. sedimentation tank

9. The hydraulic radius is defined as
   A. the distance from the center of gravity of cross-sectional area of flow to the point of minimum velocity
   B. the cross-sectional area of waterway divided by the wetted perimeter
   C. half the depth of flow
   D. the depth from the free surface to the point of maximum velocity

10. Water flowing from an orifice in the side of a tank strikes the ground at a point 10 feet, below the orifice and 5 feet from the tank.
    If the coefficient of velocity is 1.00, the height of water above the orifice, in feet, is MOST NEARLY
    A. .63   B. 1.73   C. 3.5   D. 7.9

11. Of the following formulas, the one that is MOST commonly used in determining the runoff from a watershed is Q =
    A. $A\frac{1.486}{M}R^{2/3}S^{1/2}$ B. Aci C. $CLH^{3/2}$ D. $AC\sqrt{RS}$

12. Maximum discharge in a circular sewer occurs when the ratio of the depth of flow to the diameter of the pipe is MOST NEARLY
    A. .5   B. .6   C. .9   D. 1.1

13. Of the following items, the one that is LEAST important in the design of a concrete pier is
    A. corrosion   B. erosion   C. scour   D. elutriation

14. Of the following items, the one which is LEAST related to the others is
    A. extensometer   B. weir
    C. piezometer   D. hook gauge

15. In a through truss bridge, a horizontal longitudinal member acting as a beam to support loads is known as a
    A. floor beam   B. portal brace
    C. lower chord   D. stringer

16. Using pipe A alone, a given tank is filled with water in 5 minutes. When pipe B is used alone, the same tank is filled in 7 minutes.
    If both pipes are used at the same time, the length of time required to fill this tank is, in minutes, MOST NEARLY
    A. 2.87   B. 2.92   C. 2.99   D. 3.05

17. In plane surveying, double meridian distances are used to compute the _____ of a traverse.
    A. latitudes and departures
    B. area
    C. error of closure
    D. corrections for magnetic declination for the sides

18. The deflection angle required to lay out a 50 ft. chord of a 3°00' circular curve is MOST NEARLY
    A. 0°45'   B. 1°45'   C. 2°30'   D. 3°45'

19. Of the following, the one that is NOT a method of locating details for topography is
    A. offset distance
    B. range line
    C. tie line
    D. string line

20. *Blocking in* is a practice followed when it is necessary to
    A. set up a transit on line between two stations
    B. prolong a line around an obstacle
    C. project a high point to the ground
    D. set a point on line by double centering

21. Of the following terms, the one that is LEAST related to the others is
    A. five level section
    B. slope stake
    C. mass diagram
    D. hydraulic fill

22. Using a given 100 foot tape, the slope distance between two points on a 2% grade is found to be 250.26. When checked later, the tape is found to be 100.02 ft. long.
    The horizontal distance between the two points is MOST NEARLY
    A. 250.21   B. 250.26   C. 250.29   D. 250.32

23. When it is impossible to balance the foresight and backsight distances, precise difference in elevations may be obtained by _____ leveling.
    A. trigonometric
    B. reciprocal
    C. stadia
    D. barometric

24. Specifications usually require that controlled concrete develop its design strength
    A. when forms are stripped
    B. in 28 days
    C. in 7 days
    D. in 2 months

25. Horizontal reinforcing in the exposed face of a cantilever retaining wall is necessary PRIMARILY to reinforce against _____ stress.
    A. tensile
    B. compressive
    C. shearing
    D. shrinkage

KEY (CORRECT ANSWERS)

1.	A	11.	B
2.	A	12.	C
3.	B	13.	D
4.	C	14.	A
5.	B	15.	D
6.	A	16.	B
7.	A	17.	B
8.	B	18.	A
9.	B	19.	D
10.	A	20.	A

21. D
22. B
23. B
24. C
25. D

EXAMINATION SECTION
TEST 1

DIRECTIONS: Each question or incomplete statement is followed by several suggested answers or completions. Select the one that BEST answers the question or completes the statement. *PRINT THE LETTER OF THE CORRECT ANSWER IN THE SPACE AT THE RIGHT.*

1. Asphalt is derived mainly

    A. as a byproduct from the production of coke
    B. from asphalt deposits seeping to the surface of the earth
    C. from the refining of crude oil
    D. from bituminous coal

    1.____

2. Cutback liquid asphalts are prepared by blending asphalt with a volatile solvent. The one of the following that is NOT used as an asphalt solvent is

    A. naphtha   B. gasoline   C. kerosene   D. toluene

    2.____

3. The primary purpose of the solvent in cutback asphalt is to allow the

    A. use of a larger size aggregate in the mix
    B. application of the asphalt at a relatively low temperature
    C. application of asphalt in wet weather
    D. application of asphalt in hot weather

    3.____

4. The thickness of the sheet asphalt on a sheet asphalt pavement is usually _____ inch(es).

    A. 1/2 inch to 3/4   B. 1 inch to 1 1/2
    C. 1 5/8 inches to 2   D. 2 1/4 inches to 3

    4.____

5. The grade of an asphalt cement is designated as AR4000.
   The AR is an abbreviation for

    A. asphalt rating   B. acid resistance
    C. aged residue   D. aging resistance

    5.____

6. An asphaltic emulsion is a suspension of asphalt in

    A. kerosene   B. gasoline   C. toluene   D. water

    6.____

7. A very light application of asphalt on an existing paved surface will promote bond between this surface and the subsequent course is known as a(n) _____ coat.

    A. prime   B. adhesion
    C. tack   D. penetrating

    7.____

8. Of the following, payment is usually made for asphalt pavements at the contract price per

    A. square inch   B. square foot
    C. square yard   D. 100 square feet

    8.____

45

9. The grade of an asphalt cement is designated AR4000. The 4000 is a measure of

   A. strength B. viscosity C. ductility D. density

10. Of the following, the geometric shape of a horizontal curve on a highway is

    A. parabolic
    B. hyperbolic
    C. circular
    D. elliptical

11. A borrow pit in highway construction is used

    A. for storing stormwater in a heavy rain
    B. for coarse aggregate in Portland cement concrete
    C. for coarse aggregate in asphalt concrete
    D. to obtain fill for embankments

12. Overhaul in highway construction is usually measured and paid for by the

    A. yard - cubic foot
    B. yard - cubic yard
    C. station - cubic foot
    D. station - cubic yard

13. A Benkelman beam is used in highway work

    A. as an indicator of the ability of a pavement to withstand loading
    B. to measure the roughness of an asphalt concrete pavement
    C. to measure the uniformity of an asphalt concrete pavement
    D. to measure the ability of an asphalt concrete pavement to remain serviceable if the subgrade is undermined

14. When surfacing over an existing pavement, of the following, the MOST practical way to insure that the required thickness of new pavement is met is

    A. expansion of clay when exposed to water
    B. expansion of soil when excavated
    C. waviness in a soil embankment when being compacted with a roller
    D. expansion of loamy soil when exposed to water

15. When surfacing over an existing pavement, of the following, the MOST practical way to insure that the required thickness of new pavement is met is

    A. have wood blocks of the thickness of the new pavement temporarily placed on the existing pavement to insure that the thickness requirements will be met at the time of paving
    B. make a survey of the existing pavement elevations and a survey of the final pavement elevations and check that the thickness requirements are met
    C. check that the amount of asphalt delivered is adequate to meet the depth requirements of the area to be paved
    D. take core borings to determine if the thickness meets specifications

16. The maximum roller speed for steel tired rollers paving asphalt concrete is a maximum of _____ mile(s) per hour.

    A. 7 B. 5 C. 3 D. 1

17. The weathered or dry surface appearing on a relatively new pavement can generally be attributed to

    A. inadequate rolling
    B. oversized coarse aggregate in the mix
    C. excessive amount of fine aggregate
    D. insufficient asphalt in the mix

18. Construction contracts for highways have items paid either by unit price or lump sum. The one of the following that is usually a lump sum item on a highway contract is

    A. excavation   B. paving
    C. fencing   D. demolition

19. Highway roadway subgrades are usually required to have a relative density of _____ percent.

    A. 80 to 84   B. 85 to 89   C. 90 to 95   D. 100

20. A *profile* of a highway is

    A. the section taken along the centerline of the highway
    B. an aesthetic landscape sketch of the highway
    C. used to determine the line of the highway
    D. used to locate overpasses

21. A culvert as used under a highway is usually installed

    A. as a relief sewer
    B. as a bypass for a stream
    C. in a stream bed
    D. to carry sanitary and storm flow

22. A mass diagram as related to highway construction work is used to

    A. minimize traffic congestion
    B. compute payment for hauling excavation and fill
    C. find the largest feasible radius of curvature for a horizontal curve
    D. help determine the depth of an asphalt concrete pavement

23. The geometric shape of a vertical curve on a highway is a(n)

    A. parabola   B. hyperbola   C. circle   D. ellipse

24. When cast iron bell and spigot pipe is used in sewer construction, the joint is usually sealed with

    A. lead   B. tin
    C. cement mortar   D. oakum

25. A planimeter is used to measure

    A. location   B. area   C. elevation   D. angles

KEY (CORRECT ANSWERS)

1. C
2. D
3. B
4. B
5. C

6. D
7. C
8. B
9. B
10. C

11. D
12. D
13. A
14. B
15. A

16. C
17. D
18. D
19. C
20. A

21. C
22. B
23. A
24. A
25. B

TEST 2

DIRECTIONS: Each question or incomplete statement is followed by several suggested answers or completions. Select the one that BEST answers the question or completes the statement. *PRINT THE LETTER OF THE CORRECT ANSWER IN THE SPACE AT THE RIGHT.*

1. A witness stake is usually used in surveying primarily as   1.____

    A. proof that a given location has been surveyed
    B. an aid in locating a surveying stake
    C. a marker to prevent a stake being disturbed
    D. an offset stake

2. Before the contractor begins work on a sewer or highway project, a detailed survey is made of all existing structures that may be affected by the construction in order to   2.____

    A. protect against false claims for damage
    B. insure that the contractor causes no damage to property
    C. insure that existing elevations conform to elevations on the contract drawings
    D. uncover potential weaknesses in structures

3. The optimum moisture content of a given soil will result in the   3.____

    A. plastic limit of the soil is reached
    B. liquid limit of the soil is reached
    C. porosity of the soil is at its maximum
    D. soil is compacted to its maximum dry density

4. The letters SC for soil means   4.____

    A. silty clay   B. clayey sand
    C. sandy clay   D. clayey silt

5. A cradle is used under a large precast circular concrete pipe sewer. The purpose of the cradle is mainly to   5.____

    A. minimize the settlement of the earth on the sides of the sewer
    B. minimize the settlement under the pipe
    C. strengthen the pipe against collapse
    D. resist side pressure against the pipe

6. The joints on laid precast concrete pipe were poorly made.
The consequence of this poor workmanship is most likely   6.____

    A. the pipe will settle
    B. the pipe may collapse
    C. the water table may be adversely affected
    D. there will be excessive infiltration

7. An existing sewer is to connect into a new deep manhole for a new sewer. According to old plans for the existing sewer, the elevation of the existing sewer is 1/2 inch lower than shown on the plan.
Of the following, the BEST action that the inspector can take is   7.____

A. call his superior for instructions
B. do nothing
C. have the contractor relay the existing pipe to the theoretical elevation shown on the old plan
D. have an adjustable connection placed between the old pipe and the new manhole

8. The contractor proposes using a cement-lime mix for cement mortar to be used in building a manhole.
This is

   A. *good* practice as this is a more workable mortar
   B. *good* practice as the mortar is slow setting
   C. *poor* practice because the mortar weakens in a wet environment
   D. *poor* practice as a cement-lime mortar is more porous than a cement mortar

9. Most serious claims for extra payment on large sewer contracts result from

   A. soil conditions that are markedly different from those that were presented by the owner
   B. the inspectors being unreasonable in their demands
   C. delay in making the areas available for work
   D. the fact that the method of construction required by the owner proved to be unworkable

10. Unconsolidated fill is at pipe laying depth. Of the following, the BEST action that an inspector can take is to

    A. have the unconsolidated fill removed and replaced with concrete
    B. have the unconsolidated fill removed and replaced with sound fill
    C. report this matter to your supervisor for his consideration
    D. ask the contractor to consolidate the fill

11. Buried debris not shown on the borings is uncovered near the surface of an excavation for a deep sewer. Of the following, the BEST action for an inspector to take is to

    A. record the depth and extent of the debris in the event of a claim
    B. do nothing as this has no effect on the final product
    C. notify the contractor that there is no valid claim for the extra work required
    D. be certain that the debris is not used in the backfill

12. A come-along or deadman is sometimes used in the laying of large precast concrete pipe to insure

    A. the pipe is at proper grade
    B. the pipe is on proper line
    C. that the pipe will not subsequently settle
    D. that the pipe is properly seated

13. In laying sewers,

    A. accuracy in the line of the sewer is more important than accuracy in the grade of the sewer
    B. accuracy in the grade of the sewer is more important than accuracy in the line of the sewer

C. accuracy in the line and grade of the sewer are equally important
D. since the sewer is underground, accuracy is not required either for line or grade

14. A sewer contract is given out with a price per foot of sewer for different diameter sewers. After the contract is let, the low bidder is required to give a breakdown of his price per foot of sewer to include excavation, sewer in place, backfill, and restoration. The purpose of this breakdown is to

   A. facilitate partial payments
   B. insure the bid is not unbalanced
   C. enable the agency to gather up-to-date cost data for future projects
   D. make it easier to price extra work

15. The house sewer runs from the house to the main line sewer. The size of this sewer is most frequently _____ inches.

   A. 4   B. 5   C. 6   D. 8

16. A line on centerline at the inside bottom of a pipe or conduit is known as the

   A. convert   B. invert   C. subvert   D. exvert

17. One of the most important elements of excavating for sewer construction is to maintain the specified width of the trench at the top of the pipe. If the width at the top of the pipe is too great,

   A. this may cause excessive settlement of the pipe
   B. this may cause excessive settlement of the backfill damaging the final pavement
   C. this may place excessive load on the pipe
   D. it may undermine utilities adjacent to the pipe

18. Wellpoints are used in sewer construction mainly to

   A. keep water out of the trench due to a heavy rainstorm
   B. keep water out of the excavation and subsoil to avoid excessive pressure on the sheeting
   C. prevent a boil from forming in the trench
   D. lower the water table to facilitate construction of the sewer

19. When a trench excavation uses soldier beams and horizontal sheeting for support, the minimum number of braces for each soldier beam is

   A. 1   B. 2   C. 3   D. 4

20. Bell and spigot pipe should be laid _____ with the bell end pointed _____.

   A. downstream; upstream   B. downstream; downstream
   C. upstream; upstream   D. upstream; downstream

21. The specifications state that house sewers should be laid at a grade of not less than 2%. In 40 feet of house sewer, the change in grade for 40 feet should be most nearly _____ inches.

   A. 8   B. 8 1/2   C. 9   D. 9 1/2

22. Two percent grade on a house sewer is equal to most nearly _____ inch per foot.   22._____

    A. 1/8   B. 3/16   C. 1/4   D. 5/16

23. When working underground in spaces that are closed and confined, such as manholes, the gas that is dangerous and most likely of the following to be present is   23._____

    A. carbon monoxide   B. carbon dioxide
    C. ammonia   D. methane

24. Of the following, air entrained cement would most likely be used in   24._____

    A. concrete roadways
    B. precast concrete pipe
    C. precast concrete manholes
    D. the cradle for precast concrete pipe

25. A slump cone is filled to overflowing in _____ layer(s).   25._____

    A. one   B. two separate
    C. three separate   D. four separate

KEY (CORRECT ANSWERS)

1.	B	11.	A
2.	A	12.	D
3.	D	13.	B
4.	B	14.	A
5.	B	15.	C
6.	D	16.	B
7.	B	17.	C
8.	C	18.	D
9.	A	19.	B
10.	C	20.	C

    21. D
    22. C
    23. D
    24. A
    25. C

EXAMINATION SECTION
TEST 1

DIRECTIONS: Each question or incomplete statement is followed by several suggested answers or completions. Select the one that *BEST* answers the question or completes the statement. *PRINT THE LETTER OF THE CORRECT ANSWER IN THE SPACE AT THE RIGHT.*

1. In a modification of the conventional activated sludge process known as Modified Aeration, the percentage of returned sludge to the aeration tank is, MOST nearly, 1.____

    A. 10   B. 20   C. 30   D. 40

2. The amount of chlorine, in pounds per million gallons, to produce 0.5 ppm residual in most primary effluents will, *most nearly,* be between 2.____

    A. 10 to 40   B. 50 to 70   C. 100 to 200   D. 300 to 500

3. In a conventional activated sludge treatment plant, air is applied at a rate of, most *nearly,* 3.____

    A. 1 to 1 1/2 cubic feet per gallon of sewage
    B. 3 to 3 1/2 cubic feet per gallon of sewage
    C. 4 to 5 1/2 cubic feet per gallon of sewage
    D. 7 to 7 1/2 cubic feet per gallon of sewage

4. Of the following temperature ranges, the *one* which is the *MOST* efficient for sludge digester operation is 4.____

    A. 45° F and 50° F   B. 55° F and 65° F
    C. 70° F and 75° F   D. 85° F and 95° F

5. The sewage detention time in an aeration tank using modified aeration is, *most nearly,* 5.____

    A. 2 hours   B. 4 hours   C. 6 hours   D. 8 hours

6. The BTU per cubic foot value of sludge gas from a well established and properly operated digestion tank is, most *nearly,* 6.____

    A. 150   B. 350   C. 450   D. 650

7. BOD is an abbreviation for 7.____

    A. Bacteria Operating Demand
    B. Biosorption Operating Demand
    C. Biochemical Oxygen Demand
    D. Biofilter Oxygen Demand

8. The one of the following that is normally used to control the flow of sewage to the treatment plant from the intercepting sewer is the 8.____

    A. float valve   B. sluice gate
    C. gate valve   D. regulator gate

9. A sludge gas encountered at sewage treatment plants that is corrosive and damaging to metals is

   A. carbon dioxide
   B. ethane
   C. nitrogen
   D. hydrogen sulphide

10. When sludge is withdrawn from a sludge gas collector tank with a fixed color, a compensating volume of fresh sludge or water or gas must be put into the tank to prevent the development of

    A. leakage
    B. positive pressures
    C. negative pressures
    D. condensation

11. Devices in sewage treatment plants whose function is to break or cut up solids found in sewage are known as

    A. barmimutors
    B. diffusers
    C. tricklers
    D. grinders

12. The sludge treatment process whereby the volume of sludge going to the digester is reduced is known as

    A. thickening
    B. elutriation
    C. chemical conditioning
    D. wet oxidation

13. *Most* of the suspended solids are separated or removed from the sewage by

    A. aeration   B. washing   C. elutriation   D. sedimentation

14. The *one* of the following that is usually operated by compressed air is a

    A. reducer
    B. baffle
    C. sump pump
    D. sewage ejector

15. The *PRIMARY* function of a grit chamber in a sewage treatment plant is to remove

    A. paper   B. worms   C. gravel   D. algae

16. A deep two-storied storage sewage tank with an upper sedimentaton chamber and a lower chamber is known as a _____ tank.

    A. detritus   B. imhoff   C. septic   D. elocculating

17. The *one* of the following which *BEST* characterizes activated sludge is that it is

    A. black in color and has small particles
    B. blue in color and has large particles
    C. brown in color and has some dissolved oxygen
    D. beige in color and has a great amount of dissolved oxygen

18. The *optimum* PH value of the sludge in a digester should be

    A. 10   B. 7   C. 3   D. 2

19. In the Activated Sludge Process, the *one* of the following steps that may be taken to prevent or control sludge bulkings is to

    A. decrease aeration in time and rate
    B. chlorinate returned activated sludge

C. increase the solids content carried in aeration tanks
D. raise the pH value to 7.8

20. In starting a digester unit, the QUICKEST results can be obtained by

    A. seeding   B. shredding   C. dosing   D. chlorinating

21. Sludge digestion carried out in the absence of free oxygen is known as

    A. wet oxidation   B. heat drying
    C. anaerobic decomposition D. aerobic decomposition

22. "Frothing" is MOST frequently attributable to

    A. short circuiting of aeration tanks
    B. septic sewage in primary tank
    C. high concentration of fungus
    D. detergent compounds in the sewage

23. The process of removing floating grease or scum from the surface of sewage in a tank is called

    A. squeegeeing   B. siphoning
    C. skimming   D. sloughing

24. Of the following, the one which BEST represents a primary treatment device for sewage is the

    A. stabilization pond   B. intermittent sand filter
    C. septic tank   D. aeration tank

25. Freshly poured concrete surfaces normally exposed to air should be cured for a minimum period of

    A. 4 days   B. 5 days   C. 6 days   D. 7 days

26. One of your men on the job is injured at a work site and is unconscious. The BEST course of action for you to follow is to

    A. give him liquids to drink
    B. have him remain in a lying position until medical help arrives
    C. immediately move him to the first-aid station
    D. attempt to arouse him to consciousness by shaking him

27. The type of portable fire extinguisher that is MOST effective in controlling a fire around live electrical equipment is the

    A. foam type   B. soda-acid type
    C. carbon-dioxide type   D. water type

28. The hazards of electric shock resulting from operation of a portable electric tool in a damp location can be reduced by

    A. grounding the tool
    B. holding the tool with one hand
    C. running the tool at low speed
    D. using a baffle

29. The *one* of the following that is the *proper* first aid to administer to a conscious person suffering from chlorine inhalation is

    A. an alocholic drink
    B. black coffee
    C. a pulmotor
    D. a cold shower

30. Of the following actions, the *best one* to take *FIRST* after smoke is seen coming from an electric control device is to

    A. shut off the power to it
    B. call the main office for advice
    C. look for a wiring diagram
    D. throw water on it

KEY (CORRECT ANSWERS)

1.	A	16.	B
2.	C	17.	C
3.	A	18.	B
4.	D	19.	B
5.	A	20.	A
6.	D	21.	C
7.	C	22.	D
8.	B	23.	C
9.	D	24.	C
10.	C	25.	D
11.	A	26.	B
12.	A	27.	C
13.	D	28.	A
14.	D	29.	B
15.	C	30.	A

TEST 2

DIRECTIONS: Each question or incomplete statement is followed by several suggested answers or completions. Select the one that BEST answers the question or completes the statement. PRINT THE LETTER OF THE CORRECT ANSWER IN THE SPACE AT THE RIGHT.

1. Of the following, the BEST fastener to use when attaching a pipe support bracket to a concrete wall is a(n)

    A. toggle bolt
    B. expansion bolt
    C. carriage bolt
    D. lag bolt

2. The MAIN reason for mixing a "thinner" into paint is to

    A. *clear up* air bubbles
    B. *stop* the paint from bleeding
    C. *spread* the paint easily
    D. *make* the paint color lighter

3. Schedule 40 pipe is a designation for

    A. asbestos cement pipe
    B. steel pipe
    C. transite pipe
    D. clay pipe

4. The function of a check valve in a pipeline is to

    A. relieve excessive pressure
    B. remove air
    C. meter the flow
    D. prevent reverse flow

5. The device on an electric motor which will prevent overheating is called a

    A. rheostat
    B. bus bar
    C. solenoid
    D. thermal relay

6. The oil recommended for the gear box of a 20-ton sewage plant crane is, *most nearly,*

    A. SAE 80   B. SAE 120   C. SAE 160   D. SAE 200

7. Where pump ball bearings may be subjected to water washing, the lubricating grease should have a

    A. white lead base
    B. red lead base
    C. sodium soap base
    D. lithum soap base

8. A chlorine leak can normally be detected by

    A. a lighted candle
    B. its smell
    C. a dry rag
    D. an oil-soaked rag

9. The moving wooden planks in a tank used to scrape sludge from the bottom of a tank are known as

    A. cleats   B. flights   C. rails   D. levers

10. A device with an edge or notch used for measuring liquid flow is known as a

    A. Parshall Flume
    B. Plainer Bowlus
    C. Venturi
    D. Weir

11. The *one* of the following types of pumps that is WIDELY used for pumping sewage is   11.___

    A. reciprocating   B. rotary   C. simplex   D. centrifugal

12. Prior to starting a newly installed pump, you should   12.___

    A. open the motor disconnect switch
    B. expose the pump to outside weather conditions
    C. turn the shaft by hand to see that it rotates freely
    D. disconnect the vent and drain the plugs

13. A maintenance program for a new piece of operating equipment should BEST be set up in accordance with the   13.___

    A. location of the unit
    B. location of personnel
    C. manufacturer's recommendations
    D. monthly plant capacity

14. The *one* of the following fasteners that has threads at *both* ends is called a   14.___

    A. screw   B. stud   C. blivet   D. drift bolt

15. The *one* of the following that is installed between two pipe flanges to seal the connection is called a   15.___

    A. sheave   B. gasket   C. boss   D. fillet

16. A wet undigested sludge containing a large amount of grease will MOST probably   16.___

    A. clog the opening of the filter
    B. have no effect on the efficiency of the filters
    C. cause rapid deterioration of the filter
    D. cause the filter to shrink and snap

17. The floating cover for a sludge gas storage tank is kept under a gauge pressure of, *most nearly,*   17.___

    A. 0 to 2 ounces   B. 3 to 5 ounces
    C. 6 to 9 ounces   D. 10 to 12 ounces

18. The tool that is used to remove the burrs from the end of 1/2" diameter steel pipe after cutting it with a pipe cutter is known as a   18.___

    A. bit   B. reamer   C. tap   D. caliper

19. Of the following common obstructions found in sewer lines, the *one* that occurs MOST frequently is   19.___

    A. roots   B. debris   C. grease   D. grit

20. The *one* of the following that is the MAIN reason for putting orders in writing is to   20.___

    A. protect the person who receives it
    B. protect the person who prepared the order
    C. make it easier to check mistakes
    D. protect the agency should something unforeseen occur

21. For records to provide an essential basis for future changes or expansions of the sewage treatment plant, the records must be

    A. accurate
    B. lengthy
    C. detailed in ink
    D. hand-written in pencil

    21.____

22. The volume, in cubic feet, of a slab of concrete that is 5'-0" wide, 6'-0" long, and 0'-6" in depth is, *most nearly,*

    A. 15.0   B. 13.5   C. 12.0   D. 10.5

    22.____

23. The sum of the following pipe lengths, 22 1/8", 7 3/4", 19 7/16", and 4 3 5/8", is:

    A. 91 7/8"   B. 92 1/16"   C. 92 1/4"   D. 92 15/16"

    23.____

24. The area in square feet of a plant floor that is 42 feet wide and 75 feet long is

    A. 3150   B. 3100   C. 3075   D. 2760

    24.____

25. Of the following types of gauges, the *one* that indicates pressure above and below atmospheric pressures is known as a

    A. pressure   B. vacuum   C. Bourdan   D. compound

    25.____

26. A U-tube manometer is used to measure

    A. deflection   B. height   C. radiation   D. pressure

    26.____

27. If an air-conditioning unit shorted out and caught fire, the *BEST* fire extinguisher to use would be a _____ extinguisher.

    A. water
    B. foam
    C. carbon dioxide
    D. soda acid

    27.____

28. Of the following, the *best* action to take to help someone whose eyes have been splashed with lye is to *FIRST*

    A. wash out the eyes with clean water
    B. wash out the eyes with a salt water solution
    C. apply a sterile dressing over the eyes
    D. do nothing to the eyes, but telephone for medical help

    28.____

Questions 29-30.

DIRECTIONS: Questions numbered 29 and 30 are to be answered in accordance with the information given in the following paragraph:

A sludge lagoon is an excavated area in which digested sludge is desired. Lagoon depths vary from six to eight feet. There are no established criteria for the required capacity of a lagoon. The sludge moisture content is reduced by evaporation and drainage. Volume reduction is slow, especially in cold and rainy weather. Weather and soil conditions affect concentration. The drying period ranges from a period of several months to several years. After the sludge drying period has ended, a bulldozer or tractor can be used to remove the sludge. The dried sludge can be used for fill of low ground. A filled dried lagoon can be developed into a lawn. Lagoons can be used for emergency storage when the sludge beds are full. Lagoons are popular because they are inexpensive to build and operate. They have a disadvantage of being unsightly. A hazard to lagoon operation is the possibility of draining partly digested sludge to the lagoon that creates a fly and odor nuisance.

29. In accordance with the given paragraph, sludge lagoons have the *disadvantage* of being   29.____

   A. unsightly
   B. too deep
   C. concentrated
   D. wet

30. In accordance with the given paragraph, moisture content is *reduced* by   30.____

   A. digestion
   B. evaporation
   C. oxidation
   D. removal

KEY (CORRECT ANSWERS)

1.	B	16.	A
2.	C	17.	B
3.	B	18.	B
4.	D	19.	A
5.	D	20.	B
6.	B	21.	A
7.	D	22.	A
8.	B	23.	D
9.	B	24.	A
10.	D	25.	D
11.	D	26.	D
12.	C	27.	C
13.	C	28.	A
14.	B	29.	A
15.	A	30.	B

ENGINEERING PROBLEMS

EXAMINATION SECTION
TEST 1

DIRECTIONS: Each question or incomplete statement is followed by several suggested answers or completions. Select the one that *BEST* answers the question or completes the statement. *PRINT THE LETTER OF THE CORRECT ANSWER IN THE SPACE AT THE RIGHT.*

1. Water flows from reservoir A, elevation 100', to reservoir B through 16,100' of 12" pipe. If the friction factor f is .02 and the discharge is 3.14 ft.^{3}/sec., the elevation of the water surface in reservoir B is, in feet,

    A. 5   B. 10   C. 15   D. 20   E. 25   1.____

2. A square plate, 8' on a side, is submerged in water with the top edge parallel to the water surface and 10' below the surface.
   If the plate makes an angle of 30 with the water surface, the total pressure on the plate, in pounds, is

    A. 12,000   B. 24,000   C. 36,000   D. 48,000   E. 60,000   2.____

3. A rectangular gate 4' wide by 6' high is submerged in water with the 4' side parallel to and 2' below the surface of the water. The gate is in a vertical plane. The total pressure on one side of the gate, in pounds, is

    A. 1360   B. 2975   C. 4392   D. 5774   E. 7490   3.____

4. Using the information in the preceding problem, the distance from the top of the gate to the center of pressure is, in feet,

    A. 3.6   B. 2.7   C. 1.9   D. 3.2   E. 4.3   4.____

5. Water discharges through a turbine at the rate of 60,000 ft.^{3}/min. under a head of 100'. If the efficiency of the turbine is 70%, the horsepower developed by the turbine is

    A. 11,380   B. 7,990   C. 7,950   D. 8,320   E. 6,975   5.____

6. The horsepower required to pump 40 ft.^{3} of water per minute against a head of 30' with an efficiency of 80% is

    A. 1.97   B. 2.84   C. 2.93   D. 3.16   E. 3.23   6.____

7. A steel pipe, 48" in diameter, is subjected to an internal static pressure due to a head of 300' of water.
   The theoretical thickness of the steel, in inches, assuming an allowable stress of 18,000 #/in.^{2}, is

    A. .043   B. .069   C. .117   D. .139   E. .175   7.____

2 (#1)

8. A cylindrical steel tank, 72" in diameter, is subjected to an internal pressure caused by a 50' head of water.
   The ends of the tank are capped with hemispherical heads extending outward. The allowable tensile strength of steel is taken as 18,000 #/in.^{2}
   The theoretical thickness of the heads should be, in inches,

   A. .0198   B. .0217   C. .0286   D. .0294   E. .0303

   8.____

9. A cylindrical standpipe, 20' in diameter, has its base level with the top of a rectangular swimming pool 30' x 60' x 10' deep.
   If the swimming pool is full and the standpipe empty, the energy required to pump the water from the pool into the standpipe is, in foot pounds,

   A. 33,460,000   B. 34,791,000   C. 35,600,000
   D. 36,748,000   E. 37,800,000

   9.____

10. A U-tube connecting the inlet and thorat of a venturi is filled with oil flowing through the venturi and mercury. The specific gravity of the oil is .8, of the mercury, 13.6.
    If the difference of the mercury levels in the two legs of the U-tube is 6", the head, in feet, to be used in the venturi formula, is

    A. 4   B. 6   C. 8   D. 10   E. 12

    10.____

SOLUTIONS TO PROBLEMS

1.

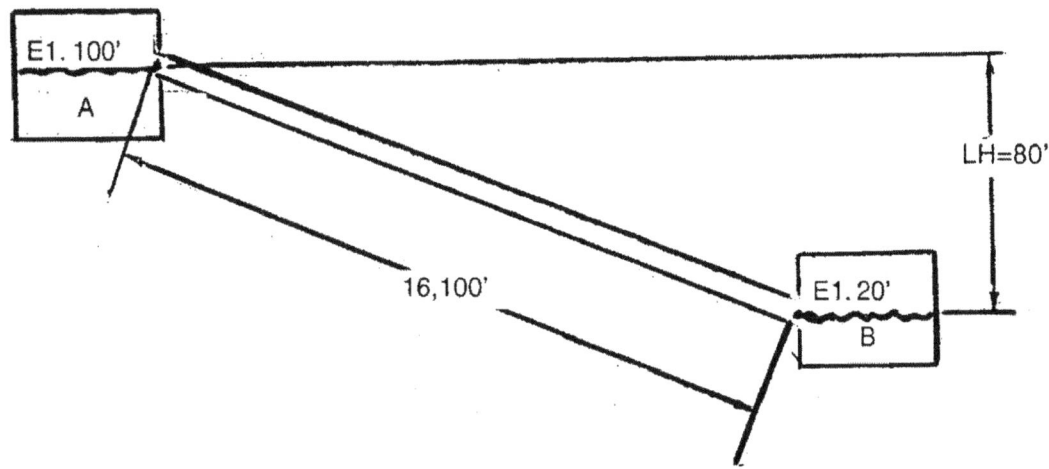

$Q = AV$
$3.14 = 3.14 \times 5^2 \times V$
$V = 4$ ft./sec

$LH = \dfrac{fLV^2}{D(2g)}$

$LH = \dfrac{.02 \times 16,100 \times 4^2}{1(2 \times 32.2)}$

$LH = 80$ ft.

LH = loss of head (ft.)
f = friction factor
L = length of pipe (ft.)
V = velocity (ft./sec.)
D = diameter of pipe (ft.)
g = constant (32.2 ft./sec.^{2})
Q = discharge (ft.^{3}/sec.)
A = cross-sectional area of pipe (ft.^{2})

The elevation of the water surface in reservoir B = 100 - 80 = 20 ft. (Answer)

2.

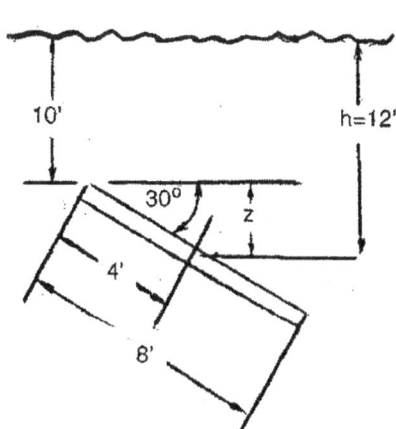 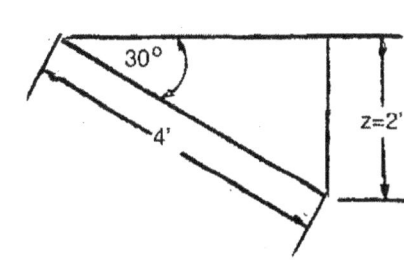

$\sin 30° = Z/4$
z = 2 ft.
h = 10 + 2 = 12 ft.
P = whA = 62.5 × 12 × 64

P = total force on one side of plate (#)
w = weight of water (62.5 #/ft.^{3})
h = distance from the top of the water surface to the centroid of the plate

4 (#1)

P = 48,000# (Answer)

3.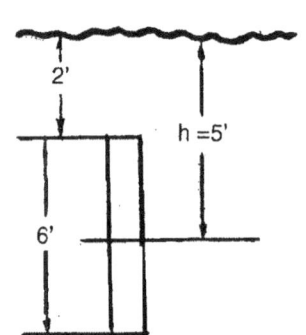

A = area of one side of plate (ft.^{2})

P = whA
P = 62.5x5x24
P = 7490# (Answer)

4.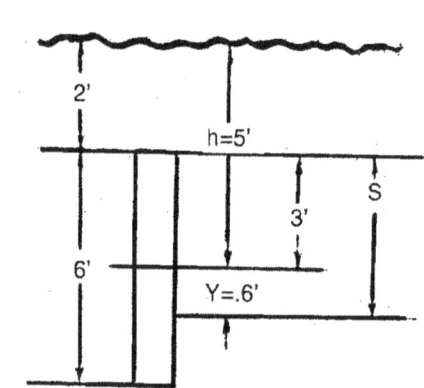

Y = distance from the centroid of the plate to the center of pressure of the plate (ft.)
I = Moment of Inertia of plate (ft.^{4})
S = distance from the top of the plate to the center of pressure (ft.)

$$I = \frac{bd^3}{12} = \frac{4 \times 6^3}{12}$$

I = 72 ft.^{4}

$$Y = \frac{I}{Ah} = \frac{72}{24 \times 5}$$

Y = .6 ft.
S = 3 + .6
S = 3.6 ft. (Answer)

5. Q = 60,000 x 1/60 = 1,000 ft.^{3}/sec.

$$HP = \frac{Qwh}{550}$$

$$HP = \frac{1,000 \times 62.5 \times 100}{550}$$

HP = 11,380 (theoretical)

Since the efficiency of the turbine is only 70%, the turbine will produce only 70% of the theoretical output or .7 x 11,380 = 7950 HP (Answer)

HP = horsepower
Q = discharge (ft.3/sec.)
h = head (ft.)
w = weight of water (62.5 #/ft.^{3})

6. Q = 40 x 1/60 = .67 ft.^{3}/sec

$$HP = \frac{Qwh}{550}$$

HP = horsepower
Q = discharge (ft.^{3}/sec)

$$HP = \frac{.67 \times 62.5 \times 30}{550}$$

h = head (ft.)
w = weight of water
    (62.5 #/ft.³)

HP = 2.27 (theoretical)

If the pump were 100% efficient, the HP required would be 2.27. Since the pump is only 80% efficient, it would produce a greater HP than the theoretical output.

The HP required to make up for the efficiency loss = $\frac{2.27}{.8}$ = 2.84 HP (Answer)

7. PD = 2 ft (formula used
      for pressure against
      a full circle)

   18,800×4 = 2×2,590,000×t

   t = .0146 ft.

   t = .0146×12 = .175 in.
       (Answer)

   P = static pressure (#/ft.²)
   D = diameter (ft.)
   f = allowable stress of steel
       (#/ft.²)
   t = thickness of pipe (ft.)
   w = weight of water (62.5 #/ft.³)
   h = head (ft.)
   P = wh = 62.5×300 = 18,800 #/ft.²
   f = 18,000×144 = 2,590,000 #/ft.²

8. P = wh = 62.5×50 = 3120 #/ft²
   f = 18,000×144 = 2,590,000
       #/ft.²
   PD = 4 ft (formula used for
        pressure against a
        hemispherical head)
   3120×6 = 4×2,590,000×t
   t = .00181 ft.
   t = .00181 × 12 = .0217 in. (Answer)

   P = static pressure (#/ft²)
   D = diameter (ft.)
   f = allowable stress of steel
       (#/ft.²)
   t = thickness of pipe (ft.)
   w = weight of water (62.5 #/ft.³)
   h = head (ft.)

9.

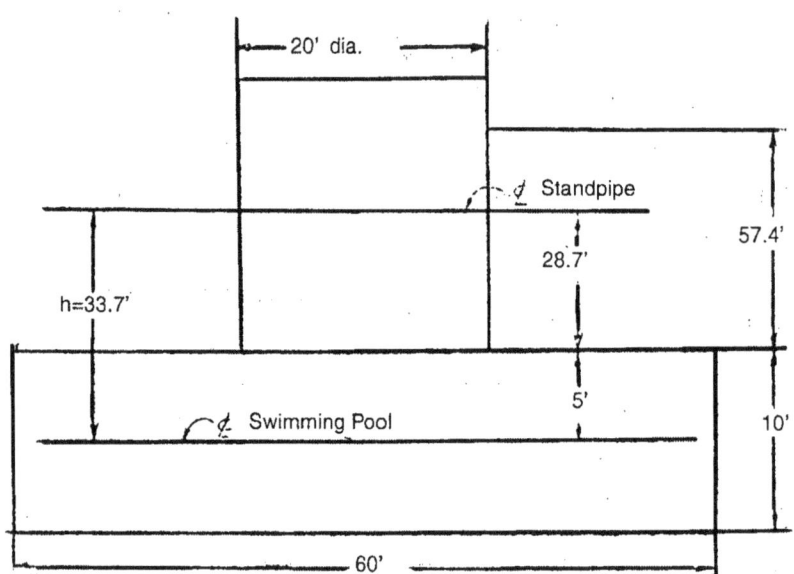

The volume of the water In the pool = 30x60x10 = 18,000 ft.^{3}.

When all the water is transferred from the pool to the standpipe, the height of the water in the standpipe is equal to

$$\frac{18,000}{\pi r^2} = 57.4 \text{ ft.}$$

$$h = \frac{10}{2} + \frac{57.4}{2} = 33.7 \text{ ft}$$

W = 18,000x62.5 = 1,125,000#
E = Wh
E = 1,125,000x33.7
E = 37,800,000 ft. # (Answer)

E = energy (ft. #)

W = total weight of water (#)

h = distance from centroid of water in pool to centroid of water In standpipe (ft.)

10.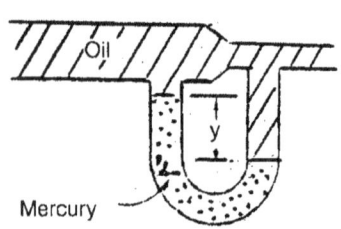

$S = \dfrac{\text{S.G. of liquid in U-tube (mercury)}}{\text{S.G. of liquid in pipe (oil)}}$

H = difference in pressure between inlet and throat (ft.)

y = difference of mercury levels (ft.)

$s = \dfrac{13.6}{.8} = 17$ H = (S - 1)y   H = (17 - 1).5   H = 8 ft. (Answer)

TEST 2

DIRECTIONS: Each question or incomplete statement is followed by several suggested answers or completions. Select the one that BEST answers the question or completes the statement. PRINT THE LETTER OF THE CORRECT ANSWER IN THE SPACE AT HE RIGHT.

1. In a specific gravity determination, the weight of a flask full of water is 390 grams. The weight of the same flask filled with water and 96.2 grams of sand is 450 grams. The specific gravity of the sand is

   A. 1.88   B. 2.03   C. 2.57   D. 2.66   E. 2.74

   1.____

2. A rectangular footing, 3'x6', in plan carries a column-load of 36,000# which acts on a line bisecting the shorter sides of the footing, 2' from one of these shorter sides. The MAXIMUM earth pressure under the footing due to this load is, in #/ft.^{2},

   A. 2,000   B. 4,000   C. 5,000.   D. 6,000   E. 8,000

   2.____

3. A dam. with a rectangular cross-section, has a width of 4'. Water stands 12' deep against one side of the dam.
   What must be the height of the dam, in feet, so that the tendency of the water to overturn it will just be counteracted? (Weight of concrete = 150 #/ft.^{3})

   A. 9   B. 12   C. 15   D. 18   E. 21

   3.____

4. A dam with a rectangular cross-section has a height of 14'. The surface of the water stands 2' below the top of the dam.
   Find the width of the dam, in feet, needed to prevent overturning. (Weight of concrete = 150 #/ft.^{3})
   The CORRECT answer is:

   A. 4.15   B. 5.39   C. 5.93   D. 6.02   E. 6.1

   4.____

5. A retaining wall, triangular in cross-section, 12' in height and 5' in width, resists a horizontal force of 1250 pounds per lineal foot of wall acting 4' above the base.
   Find the factor of safety against overturning.
   The CORRECT answer is:

   A. 1   B. 2   C. 3   D. 3.5   E. 4.5

   5.____

6. With the information given in the preceding problem, find the factor of safety against sliding if the coefficient of friction is .55.
   The CORRECT answer is:

   A. .49   B. .96   C. 1.21   D. 1.75   E. 1.98

   6.____

7. A concrete pier, 18' high, top dimensions 5'x8', has a uniform batter of 2" per foot.
   Find the volume of the pier in cubic feet.
   The CORRECT answer is:

   A. 1333   B. 1459   C. 1554   D. 1638   E. 1739

   7.____

8. A rectangular trench 6' wide (in level ground) has zero cut at Station 3 + 00 and 8.1 cut at Station 4 + 00.
Find the number of cubic yards of excavation between the two stations.
The *CORRECT* answer is:

   A. 30   B. 60   C. 90   D. 120   E. 120

9. A wooden beam, 8" wide by 12" deep, carries a uniform load of 600 pounds per foot on a simple span of 16'.
Find the MAXIMUM unit shearing stress, in pounds per in.^{2}, in the beam.
The CORRECT answer is:

   A. 15   B. 30   C. 45   D. 60   E. 75

10. The notes for a 3-level survey are:
    $$\frac{F\,6}{19} \quad \frac{F\,8}{0} \quad \frac{F\,12}{28}$$
    The width of the roadway is 20'.

    Find the area of fill in ft.^{2}.
    The CORRECT answer is:

   A. 154   B. 167   C. 210   D. 278   E. 302

SOLUTIONS TO PROBLEMS

1. $$S.G. = \frac{\text{weight of material in air}}{\text{loss of weight of material in water}}$$

   Total weight of flask (sand and water) = 450 grams
   Weight of water only = <u>390</u> grams
   Weight of sand only = 60 grams

   Weight of sand in air = 96.2 grams
   Weight of sand in water = <u>60.0</u> grams
   Loss of weight of sand in water = 36.2 grams

   $$S.G. = \frac{96.2}{36.2} = 2.66 \text{ (Answer)}$$

2.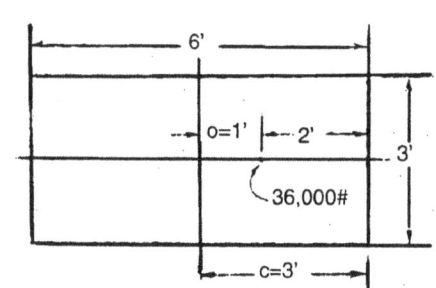

   $f = \dfrac{P}{A} + \dfrac{Pec}{I}$

   $f = \dfrac{36{,}000}{18} + \dfrac{36{,}000 \times 1 \times 3}{54}$

   $f = 4{,}000 \text{ \#/ft.}^2$ (Answer)

   f = maximum stress (#/ft.^{2})
   P = load (#)
   A = area (ft.^{2})
   e = eccentricity or distance of load from center-line of footing (ft.)
   c = the distance from the centerline of the footing to the extreme outermost fibre (ft.)
   I = Moment of Inertia (about axis which load will tend to cause rotation) (ft.^{4})
   I = bd^3/12 = 3×6^3/12 = 54 ft.^{4}

3.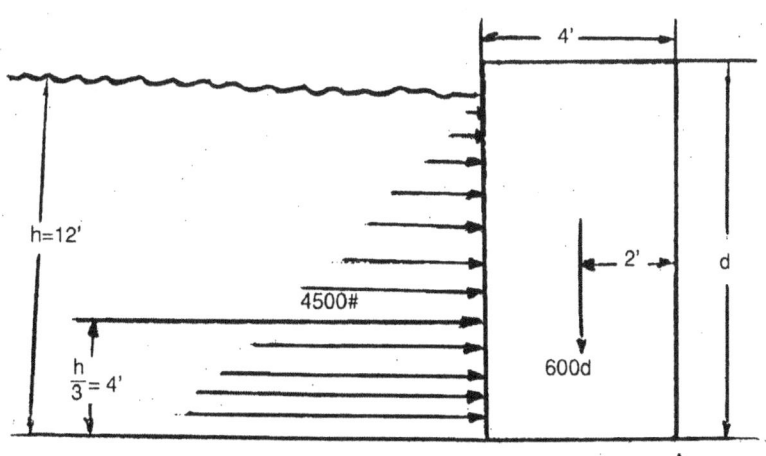

All *the* pressure of the water against the dam is considered to be acting at a point located a distance of one-third the height of the water, from the bottom.

4 (#2)

In order for the dam to just counter-act, the tendency of the water pressure to overturn it, the moment, due to the weight of the dam and the moment, due to the pressure of the water, should be equal. The dam has a tendency to overturn about point A.
NOTE: For design purposes, assume 1 ft. strip of wall.
Weight of dam = 4xdx1x150 = 600 dh=height of water (ft.)

Water Pressure = $\dfrac{wh^2}{2} = \dfrac{62.5 \times 12^2}{2}$ = 4500#   d = weight of dam (ft.)

Take moments about point A
600xdx2 = 4500x4   w = weight of water
d = 15 ft. (Answer)   (62.5#/ft.^{3})

4.

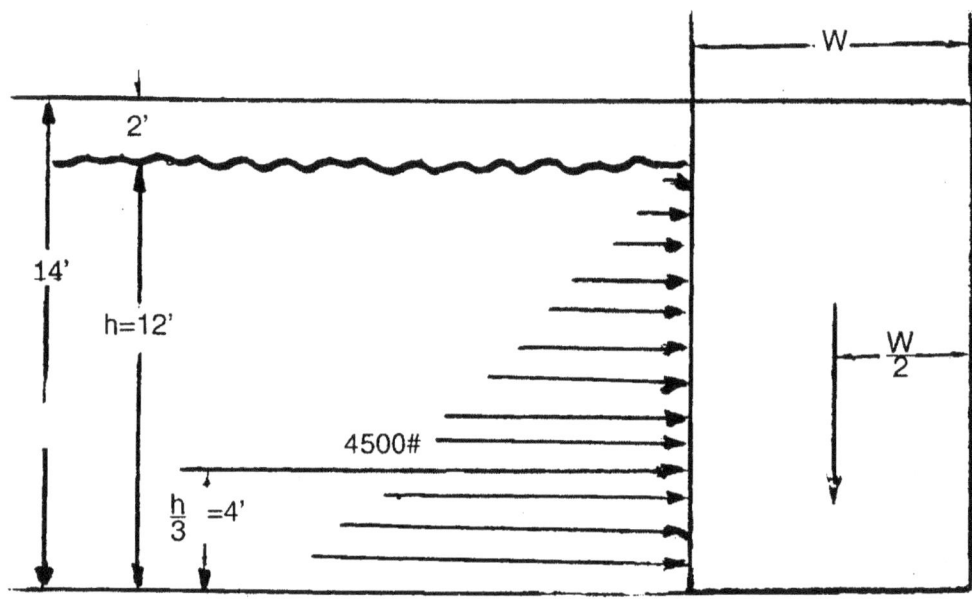

Weight of dam = 14x1xWx150 = 2100W   h = height of water (ft.)

WaterPressure = $\dfrac{wh^2}{2} = \dfrac{62.5 \times 12^2}{2}$ = 4500#   w = width of dam (ft.)

Take moments about point A
4500x4 = 2100xWxW/2   w = weight of water
                                                  (62.5 #/ft.^{3})

W = 4.15 ft. (Answer)

5. Weight of wall (1 ft. strip) =12x5/2 (1x150) = 4500#
    Horizontal Force = 1250#
    Take moments about point A
    Overturning Moment = 1250x4 = 5000 ft.#
    Restoring Moment = 4500x3.33 = 15,000 ft.#

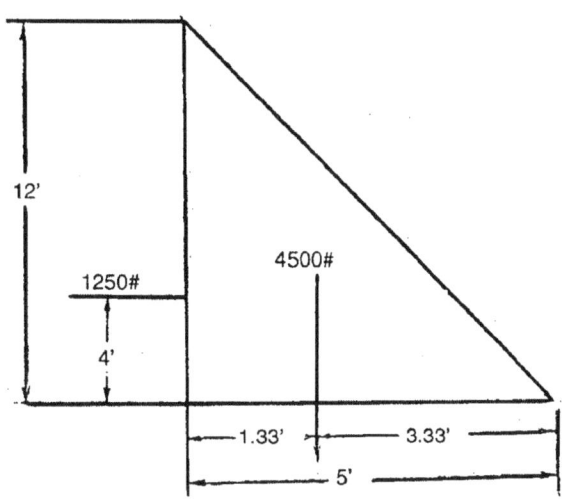

Factor of safety against overturning = $\dfrac{\text{Restoring Moment}}{\text{Overturning Moment}}$

Factor of safety = $\dfrac{15{,}000}{5{,}000}$ = 3 (Answer)

6. $F = uN$
   $F = .55 \times 4500$
   $F = 2470\#$
   Force causing sliding = 1250#

   F = frictional resistance to sliding (#)
   u = coefficient of friction
   N = normal force (weight of wall) (#)

   Factor of safety against sliding = $\dfrac{F}{\text{Force cause sliding}}$

   Factor of safety = $\dfrac{2470}{1250}$ = 1.98 (Answer)

7.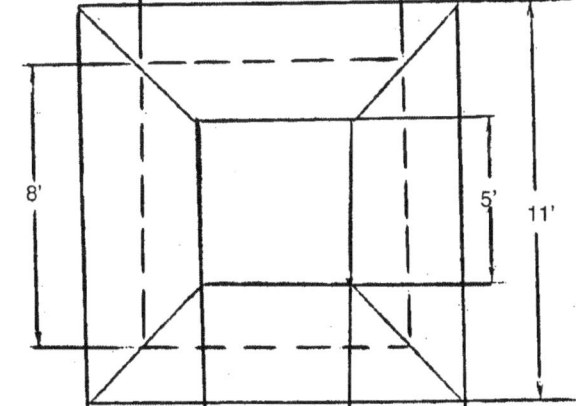

   V = volume (ft.^{3})

   L = height or length (ft.)

   A = Area of one end (ft.^{2})

   A' = Area of other end (ft.^{2})

   M = Area at mid-point (ft.^{2})

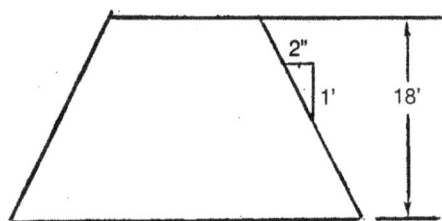

A = 5x8 = 40 ft.²
Using a batter of 2 in, per ft., the dimensions of the base of the pier will be 14 ft. by 11 ft.
A' = 14x11 = 154 ft.²
Dimensions of the mid-point can be obtained by averaging the dimensions of the top and the base of the pier.
M = 8x11 = 88 ft.²

$$V = \frac{L}{6}(A + 4M + A') = \frac{18}{6}(40 + 4 \times 88 + 154)$$

V = 1638 ft.³ (Answer)

8.

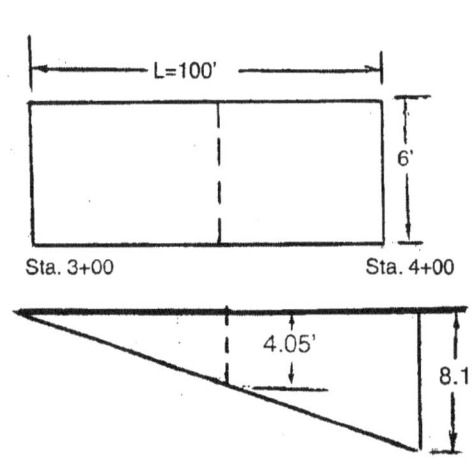

V = volume (ft.³)

L = height or length (ft.)

A = Area of one end (ft.²)

A' = Area of other end (ft.²)

H = Area at raid-point (ft.²)

L = 100 ft.   A = O
A' = 6x8.1 = 48.6 ft.²   M = 6x4.05 = 24.3 ft.²

$$V = \frac{L}{6}(A + 4M + A')$$

$$V = \frac{100}{6}(0 + 4 \times 24.3 + 48.6)$$

V = 2,430 ft.³ or $V = \frac{2,430}{27} = 90$ yds.³ (Answer)

9.

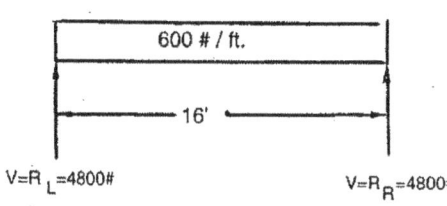

v = maximum unit shearing stress (#/in.²)

V = maximum shear (#)

b = width (in.)

d = depth (in.)

$$v = \frac{1.5V}{bd} \text{ (for homogenous beams only)}$$

$$v = \frac{1.5 \times 4800}{8 \times 12}$$

$v = 75$ #/in.² (Answer)

10.

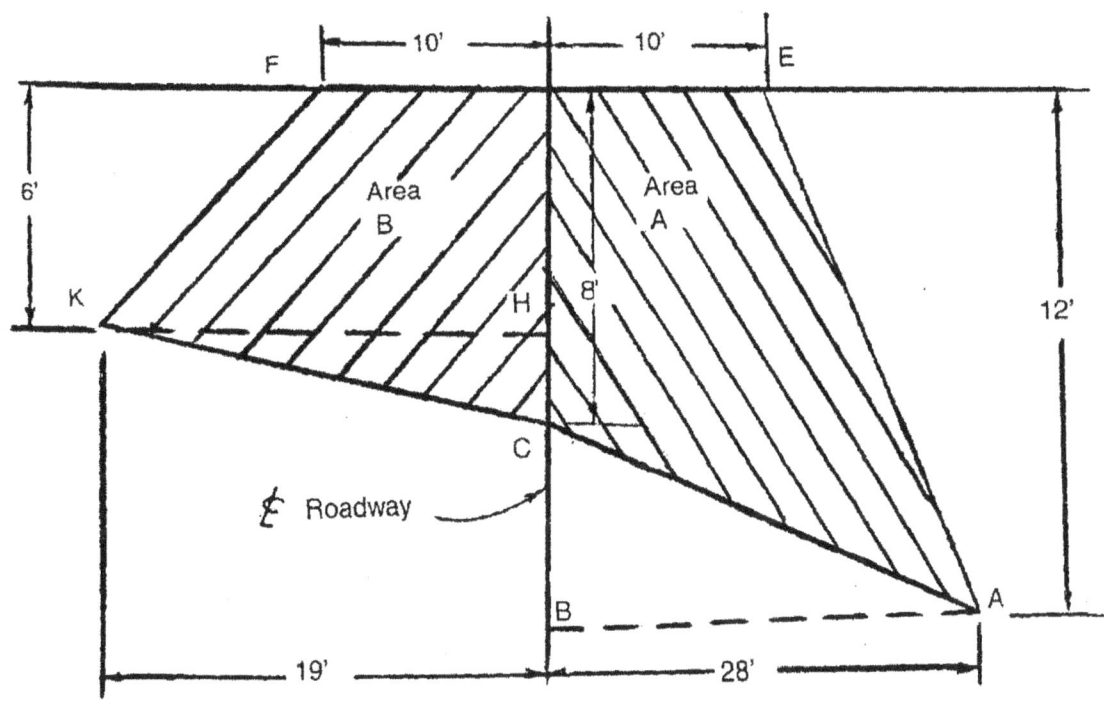

$\dfrac{12}{28}$ (fill 12 ft., 28 ft. to the right of the center-line of road)

$\dfrac{F\ 8}{0}$ (fill 8 ft. at center-line of road)

$\dfrac{F\ 6}{19}$ (fill 6 ft., 19 ft. to the left of the center-line of road)

Find Area A

Area of trapezoid $ABDE = \dfrac{10+28}{2}(12) = 228 \text{ft.}^2$

Subtract area of triangle ABC = $\dfrac{28 \times 4}{2}$ = 56 ft²

Area A = 228-56 = 172 ft.²
Find Area B

Area of trapezoid HKFD = $\dfrac{19+10}{2}$ (6) = 87 ft.²

Add area of triangle CHK = $\dfrac{19 \times 2}{2}$ = 19 ft.²

Area B = 87 + 19 = 106 ft.²
Total Fill = Area A + Area B = 172 + 106
Total Fill = 278 ft.² (Answer)

EXAMINATION SECTION
TEST 1

DIRECTIONS: Answer the following questions directly, briefly, and succinctly.

1. Air flows in a horizontal pipe. At section 1, diameter is 6 inches, pressure of the air is 30 psia, its temperature is 70° F, and its velocity is 30 feet per second. At section 2, the velocity is 200 feet per second, and the temperature is 70° F.
   If flow is steady and the temperature is constant at all points along the flow path, calculate the diameter, pressure, and density at section 2.

   1.____

2. The static temperature and pressure in a high-velocity air stream are 200° F and 40 psia, respectively.
   If the Mach No. of the stream is 0.8 and the specific-heat ratio is 1.4, determine the stagnation temperature and pressure.

   2.____

3. At the end of a concrete canal 10 feet wide, a sharp-crested weir is constructed. The weir is 8 feet high and the channel walls extend beyond the top of the weir at a height of 9.44 feet above the bottom of the canal and the nappes are completely ventilated below the weir. How much water is flowing over the weir?

   3.____

4. Water flowing from an artesian well is measured by means of a rectangular notched weir cut in a thin metal plate. The edges of the notch are clean and square. The weir notch is 2 feet high above the stream bed and 18 inches long. The sides of the notch are 6 inches high and the whole plate fills the stream channel 36 inches wide.
   What is the maximum flow capacity of the notch?

   4.____

5. Air with a specific-heat ratio of 1.4 and a Mach number of 3.0 is initially at 500° R and 20 psia. The air undergoes a one-dimensional normal shock.
   Determine the stagnation temperature downstream of the shock if the flow is adiabatic.

   5.____

6. The mass-flow rate of air (k = 1.4 and R - 53.3 foot pounds force/pound mass degree R) in a two-foot inside diameter duct is to be determined. The stagnation temperature of the air is known to be 500° R. A pressure traverse is made by means of a Pitot tube, and the average manometer deflections are found to be 24 inches and 15 inches of mercury, respectively, for the inner and outer tubes of the Pitot tube assembly. Atmospheric pressure is 29.92 inches of mercury.
   Determine the mass-flow rate of the air lb/min.

   6.____

7. At sea level, the atmospheric pressure and temperature are 14.7 psia and 70° F, respectively.
   Calculate the pressure at an altitude of 30,000 feet if it may be assumed that pressure-temperature relationships are isentropic.

   7.____

8. The flow of an ideal liquid through an orifice is assumed to be a function of the orifice diameter, the fluid density, and the pressure drop through the orifice.
   By dimensionless analysis, establish the relationship.

   8.____

2 (#1)

9. A jet discharges from a circular sharp-edged orifice 2 inches in diameter under a head of 9 feet. The discharge is measured and found to be 18.9 cu ft in a period of 1 minute. The coordinates of the center line of the jet are 8.14 ft horizontally from the orifice and 2 feet vertically below the center of orifice.
Calculate the coefficients of velocity, discharge, and contraction and the diameter of the jet at the vena contracta.

9.____

10. Water is flowing through a rectangular sharp-edged weir notch 2 ft wide, 6 inches high, and set 2 feet above the bottom of an approach channel 2 feet wide and 2 feet 6 inches deep.
If the water just fills the approach channel, how much is flowing over the weir notch? What effect does the velocity of approach have on the flow over the weir?

10.____

11. In connection with a water turbine test, the discharge water goes into a flume 3 feet wide. At the end of this flume, it is measured by a sharp-crested weir 3 feet high with no end contractions.
If the head on the weir is 3.5 feet, what is the flow in cubic feet per second that is used in the test? (The water in the flume has a normal velocity distribution.)

11.____

12. A certain spillway dam on an irrigation project has a length of 80 ft, flanked by bulkhead sections rising 8 feet above the spillway crest.
If a flood of 7600 cubic feet per second goes over the spillway, will the bulkhead sections be overtopped? (Assume the spillway coefficient to be 3.85.)

12.____

13. At an activated sludge plant, return sludge is controlled by flow over a sharp-crested triangular weir.
If the weir has a total angular opening of 90° and the sludge is 10 inches deep above the notch, how much sludge is flowing over the weir? The sludge may be assumed to flow like water at a temperature of 65° F.

13.____

14. In making a test of a small turbine, the water discharge is measured by means of a triangular weir notch that is made of smooth brass with sharp squared edges and a central angle of 90°. The water in the rectangular channel leading to the notch is 4 feet deep and 4 feet wide while the bottom of the notch is 3 feet 3 inches above the floor of the channel. What is the rate of discharge from turbine?

14.____

15. At an ice skating rink, the ice is flooded by means of a rubber hose 2 inches in diameter, 100 feet long, and ending in a nozzle with the tip 1 1/2 inches in diameter. If the nozzle is held level 3 feet above the ice by the operator, the jet strikes the ice 15 feet away.
Find the flow in the nozzle and the pressure required at the valve at the upstream end of the hose. The discharge coefficient of the nozzle may be taken as .90 and there is no contraction. The rubber hose might be assumed similar to a welded steel pipe. The kinematic viscosity may be taken as 1.2×10^{-5} square feet per second.

15.____

16. A dredge, filling in a beach, is pumping sand and water through a horizontal welded steel pipe 10 inches in diameter. The pipe is 3 ft above ground and its water and sand hit the ground 3 feet away from the end of the pipe.
How much dredged material is flowing through the pipe in gallons per minute?

16.____

17. At a water supply plant, the raw water inflow is measured by means of a venturi meter located in a pipe 20 inches in diameter. The throat of the meter is 8 inches in diameter and the discharge coefficient is 0.95.
If the difference in pressure between the upstream end and the throat is 5 psi, at what rate in gallons per minute will water flow through the meter?

17.____

18. In a water supply pipeline 10 feet in diameter, there is a level Venturi meter with a throat 5 feet in diameter. At the upper end of the meter, the internal pressure is measured by an open water manometer which rises to a height of 30 feet above the center of the pipe. The meter discharge coefficient is 0.98.
If 300 cubic feet per second of water are flowing through the meter, what would be the height of the water in the manometer at the throat?

18.____

19. How much oil in gallons per minute is flowing through a Venturi meter with a 4-inch throat placed in a pipeline 6 inches in diameter? A mercury oil differential gauge connected between the upstream section and the throat shows a difference of 8 inches. The specific gravity of oil is 0.95 and the discharge coefficient is 0.98.

19.____

20. Two sewer pipes A and B join and discharge into C, a third sewer pipe made of concrete 6 feet in diameter laid on a slope of .0006, and flowing half full. Manning's roughness coefficient n may be taken as .013 for all sewers. Sewer A is 30 in. in diameter, laid on a slope of .002 and its maximum flow carries 15 cu ft per sec. How high must the invert of sewer A be placed above sewer C so that sewage will not back up into it from the junction? How much sewage is flowing in sewer B?

20.____

21. Two sewers, A and B, of vitrified clay pipe, join and discharge into sewer C. Pipe A is 42 inches in diameter and is laid on a slope of 0.0015; the sewage flows at a depth of 30 inches. Pipe C is 60 inches in diameter and is laid on a slope of 0.0006 with its invert 10 inches below the invert of pipe A.
If the sewage levels in pipes A and C are to be the same, how much sewage may be permitted to flow in pipe B?

21.____

22. A floodway is trapezoidal in cross-section, 120 feet wide on the bottom, 180 feet on the top, and 20 feet deep below the lower chord of a bridge. One mile downstream, there is another bridge on the same channel with its lower chord 0.90 foot below that of the first bridge. What will be the capacity of the floodway if the water surface just touches the two bridges? (The channel is paved on the sides and has a gravel bottom.)

22.____

23. The sketch shows a pipe whose internal diameter is 8 inches and which has its end sealed off with a plate. The pipe conveys water, and this water leaves through a slit placed along the side of the pipe. Velocity of the water leaving the slit varies in accordance with position and is given by v = 12 + x, where v is velocity in fps and x represents the distance in feet from the beginning of the slit. Upstream of the slit, the uniform velocity in the pipe is 12 fps.
If the slit is to be 1/2 inch wide, determine the length of slit required for steady flow.

23.____

24. On a fire boat, there is a smooth brass nozzle four inches in diameter at the tip and connected to an eight-inch pipe. By means of a wheel control, the nozzle is set at an angle of 45 to the horizontal. A pressure gauge on the eight-inch pipe near the nozzle reads 25 psi. If air resistance is neglected, how high would the jet stream arise above the nozzle? How much water in gallons per minute is flowing from the nozzle? The nozzle coefficient may be taken as 0.95.

24.____

25. A concrete-lined canal has a bottom width of 32 feet with a side-slope ratio of 1 vertical to 1 1/2 horizontal.
If water runs 26 feet deep and the slope of the water surface is 1.5 inches in a half mile, how much water is flowing?

25.____

26. In an irrigation project, it is required to deliver 50 cubic feet of water per second through a rectangular (half square) concrete-lined flume from one canal to another that is 30 feet below and 2000 feet away.
What size should the flume be?

26.____

27. In order to pass a small brook under the earth fill of a new thruway, a rectangular concrete culvert (channel) was constructed 8 feet wide, 7 feet high, and 900 feet long.
If 120 cubic feet per second of water are flowing at an average depth of 5 feet in the culvert, what is the total drop of the water surface from one end to the other?

27.____

28. An irrigation canal has been provided with a bottom 20 feet wide and side slopes at 45° all lined with concrete. If the canal is 10 feet deep and delivers 1050 cfs of water, what is the necessary drop of level per mile?

28.____

29. A water supply canal is excavated in sandy earth, 120 feet wide at the bottom with side slopes of 1 vertical on 2 horizontal.
If the slope of the water surface is 3 inches per mile, how much water is flowing through the canal?

29.____

30. At the height of one of the fall floods, a river cross-section was found to be as shown in the sketch.
If the slope at the water surface was 20 feet per mile, how much water was flowing in the river?

30.____

31. A winding river with some pools and shoals has an average width of 1/2 mile, a depth of 9 feet, and the banks are fairly steep. In a one-mile distance along the river, the water surface has a drop of 2 feet. Where the river passes under a bridge, a current-meter measurement of the flow is to be made.
What flow should the current-meter indicate?

31.____

32. A combined sewer made of vitrified clay pipe 24 inches in diameter is laid on a grade of 0.4 foot drop in 100 feet. If the pipe flows half full, how much sewage is flowing? What would be the velocity and discharge if the pipe flowed full?

32.____

5 (#1)

33. A vitrified clay pipe sewer 30 inches in diameter flows half full of sanitary sewage from manhole A to manhole B 500 feet away. The invert of the sewer at the upper manhole A is at elevation 101.54 feet and at manhole B it is 99.14 feet.
How much sewage is flowing in the pipe? If charts are used in obtaining the answer, describe the procedure.

33.____

34. A nozzle is to be designed to pass 150 gpm of liquid water from a pipe to a tank. Inside the pipe, the water has a pressure of 350 psia, a temperature of 150° F, and a velocity of 8 fps. The tank is open to the atmosphere, and the corresponding pressure may be assumed to be 15 psia.
Sketch a suitable nozzle shape and calculate the minimum diameter of the nozzle. (The water may be considered to be incompressible.)

34.____

35. A very long, 2-foot inside diameter pipe is used to transport a fluid whose bulk modulus is 200,000 psi. At some unknown location along its length, the pipe becomes plugged so that no fluid can flow. In order to find the location of the plugged point, a nonleaking piston is inserted into one open end of the pipe. It is observed that the pressure of the fluid within the pipe increases 50 psi when the piston is moved a distance of 3 feet. How far away from the open end would you advise looking for the obstruction?

35.____

36. In a missile which is accelerating at a rate of 300 ft/ sec^2, a mercury U-tube manometer shows a deflection of 9 inches above ambient.
Determine the corresponding absolute pressure if the ambient pressure within the missile is 12 psia.

36.____

37. A cylindrical disc, 12 inches in diameter and 6 inches high, weighs 5 pounds. When placed in an oil-filled tube open to atmosphere, terminal velocity of the disc is noted to be 0.6 foot per second.
If the tube has an inside diameter of 12.02 inches, determine the viscosity of the oil.

37.____

38. The gate shown at the right in elevation is 2.5 meters wide into the plane of the paper. It is immersed in a fluid that weighs 10 kilonewtons per cubic meter. The total force exerted on the gate by the fluid is _____ kN.

38.____

   A. 100
   B. 200
   C. 300
   D. 400
   E. 500

39. At its maximum section below the waterline, a ship fills half the cross-sectional area of a canal.
When it moves through the canal at a speed of 5 meters per second, the mean water velocity relative to the ship at its maximum section is about _____ m/s.

39.____

   A. 20   B. 15   C. 10   D. 5   E. 2.5

40. An instrument package of mass m is to be dropped from a spacecraft to the surface of the Moon.
In order to pinpoint the location of impact, which of the following factors is LEAST important?
The

    A. latitude of the Moon at which the drop is to occur
    B. period of the Moon's rotation
    C. velocity of the package at the instant of drop
    D. gravitational acceleration for the Moon at the location of the drop
    E. mass of the package

41. The replacement of a piece of equipment is being considered.
The cost of extending the service of this equipment for 2 more years is affected by all of the following factors EXCEPT the

    A. initial investment
    B. minimum attractive rate of return
    C. operating expenses
    D. current salvage value
    E. salvage value at the end of 2 more years

SOLUTIONS TO PROBLEMS

1. CORRECT ANSWER: 29.3 psia; 0.00465 slug/cu ft; 2.35 in

$A_1 = .196$ sq ft, $T_1 = 530R$, $V_1 = 30$ fps,
$p_1 = 30$ psia
Steady Flow at T = C, $T_2 = 530R$, $V_2 = 200$ fps

Bernoulli's Equation for Isothermal and Compressible fluid flow:

$$\frac{p_1}{w_1}\log_e p_1 + \frac{V_1^2}{2g} + z_1 - H_L = \frac{p_1}{w_1}\log_e p_2 + \frac{V_2^2}{2g} + z_2$$

Given: horizontal pipe, then $z_1 = z_2$ Assume lost head, $H_L = 0$

Then: $\frac{p_1}{w_1} \times 2.3 \times \log_{10}p_1 + \frac{V_1^2}{2g} = \frac{p_1}{w_1} \times 2.3 \times \log_{10}p_2 + \frac{V_2^2}{2g}$

For Isothermal, the general gas law may be expressed as:

$$\frac{p_1}{w_1} = \frac{p_2}{w_2} = \frac{p}{w} = RT = 53.3 \times 530 = 28,250 \text{ (for air)}$$

Then: $28,250 \times 2.3 \times \log_{10}(30 \times 144) + \frac{30^2}{64.4} = 28,250 \times 2.3 \times \log_{10}p_2 + \frac{200^2}{64.4}$

A. From above equation: $\log_{10}p_2 = 3.62610$
And, p2 = 4225 psf = <u>29.3 psia</u>

B. Specific weight, $w_2 = \frac{p_2}{RT} = \frac{4225}{28,250} = 0.15$ lb/cu ft

Density, $\rho = \frac{w}{g} = \frac{0.15}{32.2} = \underline{0.00465 \text{ slug/cu ft}}$

C. From continuity of flow: $w_2 A_2 V_2 = w_1 A_1 V_1$, And, $A_2 = \frac{w_1 A_1 V}{w_2 V_2}$

$A_2 = \frac{.153 \times .196 \times 30}{.15 \times 200} = .03$ sq ft, $D_2 = \sqrt{\frac{4 \times .03 \times 144}{\pi}} = \underline{2.35 \text{ in.}}$

2. CORRECT ANSWER: 744°R; 61 psi

The following equations apply only when the Mach No. is less than unity.
Subscript ($_o$) = stagnation conditions.
No subscript = static conditions.

Stagnation Temperature, $T_o = T \times (1 + \frac{k-1}{2} \times M^2)$

$= 660 \times (1 + \frac{1.4-1}{2} \times 0.8^2) = \underline{744° R}$

Stagnation Pressure, $P_0 = p \times (1 + \frac{k-1}{2} \times M^2)^{\frac{k}{k-1}}$

$= 40 \times (1 + \frac{1.4-1}{2} \times 0.8^2)^{3.5} = \underline{61\text{psi}}$

The following relationship holds for adiabatic flow:

$\frac{T_0}{T} = (\frac{P_0}{p})^{\frac{k-1}{k}}$

3. CORRECT ANSWER: 57.6 cfs

The Francis Formula for discharge over a sharp-edged rectangular weir is:

$Q = 3.33(b - \frac{nH}{10})[(H + \frac{V_0^2}{2g})^{3/2} - (\frac{V_0^2}{2g})^{3/2}]$

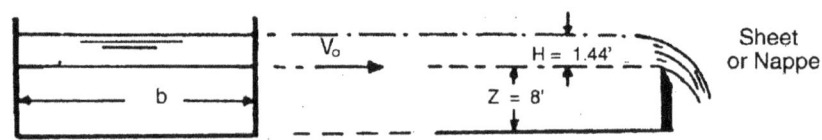

Area of Channel of Approach, $A_c = 10 \times 9.44 = 94.4$ sq ft

Where: b = length of the weir crest in feet
      H = head on the crest of weir in feet. Upstream to avoid curvature
      V_0 = average velocity of approach in channel upstream from weir
      n = number of contractions = 0 for a suppressed weir
                                                        = 1 for weir with one contraction
                                                        = 2 for fully contracted weir

The crest of the weir must be horizontal and atmospheric pressure maintained under the nappe.

Solution: The sides of the channel extend beyond the crest so the number of contractions is zero and the weir is suppressed. n = 0

Since both Q and V_0 are unknown, first calculate a trial value of Q assuming V_0 is negligible.

$Q = 3.33 b H^{3/2} = 3.33 \times 10 \times 1.44^{3/2} = 57.6 \text{ cfs}$

$V_0 = \frac{Q}{A_c} = \frac{57.6}{10 \times 9.44} = .61 \text{fps}$ And, $\frac{V_0}{2g}$ is negligible.

Since the velocity head is negligible, then Q = $\underline{57.6 \text{ cfs}}$

If the velocity of approach were not negligible, then the flow would be:

$$Q = 3.33b[(H + \frac{V_0^2}{2g})^{3/2} - (\frac{V_0^2}{2g})^{3/2}]$$

4. CORRECT ANSWER: 1.65 cfs

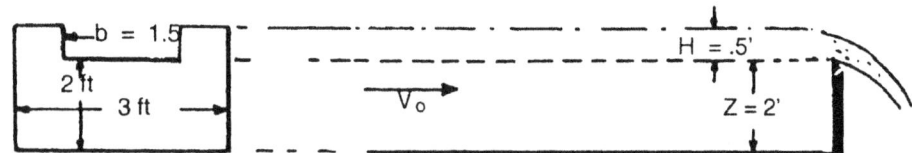

This weir may be assumed to be a fully contracted weir because the sides of the channel do not extend beyond the crest of the weir. n = 2

Assume no velocity of approach and maximum head over crest of weir.

$Q = 3.33(b - .2H) \times H^{3/2} = 3.33(1.5 - .2 \times .5) \times .5^{3/2} = 1.65$ cfs

$V = \frac{Q}{A_c} = \frac{1.65}{3 \times 2.5} = .22$ fps AND, $\frac{V_0^2}{2g} = \frac{.22^2}{64.4} = .00075$ ft neligible

Maximum flow capacity: Q = <u>1.65 cfs</u>

5. CORRECT ANSWER: 1400°R

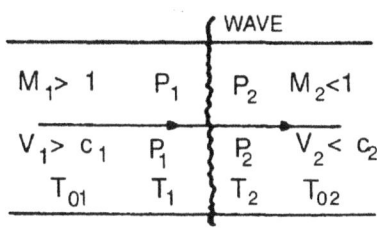

The normal shock wave occurs in gases with abrupt reduction from supersonic to sonic velocity and is accompanied by large and abrupt rises in pressure, density, temperature, and entropy.

$M_1 = 3$, $p_1 = 20$ psia, and, $T_1 = 500°R$

The following relationships hold:

$M_2^2 = \frac{(k-1)M_1^2 + 2}{2kM_1^2 - (k-1)} = \frac{(1.4-1) \times 3^2 + 2}{2 \times 1.4 \times 3^2 - (1.4-1)} = .226$ AND, $M_2 = .475$

Acoustic velocity, $c_1 = \sqrt{KGRT_1} = \sqrt{1.4 \times 32.2 \times 53.3 \times 500} = 1095$ fps
Actual velocity, $V_1 = c_1 M_1 = 1095 \times 3 = 3285$ fps

Actual velocity, $V_2 = V_1 \frac{(k-1)M_1^2 + 2}{(k+1)M_1^2} = 3285 \times \frac{(1.4-1) \times 3^2 + 2}{(1.4-1) \times 3^2} = 852$ fps

Acoustic velocity downstream, $c_2 = \frac{V_2}{M_2} = \frac{852}{.475} = 1795$ fps

Then: $1795 = \sqrt{KGRT_2} = \sqrt{1.4 \times 32.2 \times 53.3 \times T_2}$ AND, $T_2 = 1340°R$

Stagnation temp., $T_{o2} = T_2 \times (1 + \frac{k-1}{2} \times M_2^2) = 1340(1 + \frac{.4}{2} \times .226) = \underline{1400°R}$

6. CORRECT ANSWER: 17,200 lb/min

The inner tube of the Pitot tube assembly measures stagnation gage pressure.
The outer tube measures static gage pressure.
Mercury, w_g = .492 lb/cu in

Static pressure, $p = w_g h = 0.492 \times (15 + 29.92) = 22.05$ psia

Stagnation pressure, $p_0 = 0.492 \times (24 + 29.92) = 26.49$ psia

For adiabatic flow: $T_o = T \times (\frac{p_o}{p})^{\frac{k-1}{k}}$ Or, $500 = T(\frac{26.49}{22.05})^{.286} = T\, 1.056$

Static temperature, $T = 474°$ R
Specific weight of air for static conditions,

$$w = \frac{p \times 144}{RT} = \frac{22.05 \times 144}{53.3 \times 474} = 0.1257 \text{ lb / cu ft}$$

Acoustic velocity, $c = \sqrt{KgRT} = \sqrt{1.4 \times 32.2 \times 53.3 \times 474} = 1057$ fps

Then: $\frac{p_o}{p} = (1 + \frac{k-1}{2} \times M^2)^{\frac{k}{k-1}}$ or, $\frac{26.49}{22.05} = (1 + \frac{1.4-1}{2} \times M^2)^{.286}$

Or, $1.21^{3.5} = (1 + .2M^2)$ And, $M = .688$
Then: $V = cM = 1057 \times .688 = 727$
Mass Flow Rate, $G = wAV = (.1257 \times 3.14 \times 727) \times 60 = \underline{17{,}200 \text{ lb/min.}}$

7. CORRECT ANSWER: 4.14 psia

The pressure-height relation for the general case, the polytropic, is:

$$z_2 - z_1 = \frac{n}{n-1} \times RT_1 \times [1 - (\frac{p_2}{p_1})^{\frac{n-1}{n}}]$$

$n = k = 1.4$ for dry adiabatic atmosphere. $R = 53.3$

$$30{,}000 = \frac{1.4}{1.4-1} \times 53.3 \times 530 \times [1 - (\frac{P_2}{14.7})^{\frac{1.4-1}{1.4}}] =$$

$$98{,}900 - 98{,}900\, (\frac{P_2}{14.7})^{.286}$$

$P_2^{.286} = 14.7^{.286} \times \frac{68{,}900}{98{,}900} = 1.5$ And, $P_2 = 4.14$ psia

8. CORRECT ANSWER: $KD^2 \times \sqrt{\frac{p}{\rho}}$

Flow, Q = function of density ρ, pressure p and orifice diameter $Q = f(\rho, p, D) = \rho^a p^b D^c$
In terms of force F, length L, and time T:
$\rho = FT^2L^{-4}$, $p = FL^{-2}$, $D = L$

11 (#1)

Then: $F^0L^3T^1 = (FT^2L^{-4})^a(FL^{-2})^b(L)^C = (F^aT^{2a}L^{-4a})(F^bL^{-2b})(L^C)$

$a + b = 0$, $-4a - 2b - c = 3$, $-1 = 2a$, $a = -\frac{1}{2}$, $b = \frac{1}{2}$ and $c = 2$

$$Q = K\rho^{\frac{1}{2}}P^{\frac{1}{2}}D^2K = KD^2 \times \sqrt{\frac{P}{\rho}}$$

9. CORRECT ANSWER: 0.96; 0.600; 0.625; 1.58 inches

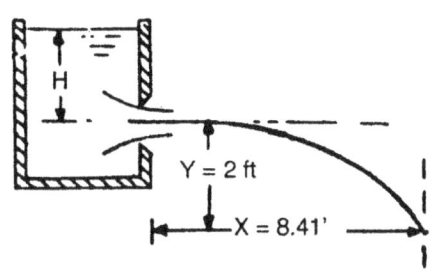

Equations of motion:
Horizontal, $X = Vt$
Vertical, $Y = \frac{1}{2}gt^2$
Eliminating t from these equations:
Actual Velocity at jet, $V = X\sqrt{\frac{g}{2y}}$
Ideal Vel. $V_i = \sqrt{2gH} = \sqrt{64.4 \times 9} = 24.1$ fps

Actual Vel., $V = X\sqrt{\frac{g}{2y}} = 8.14 \times \sqrt{\frac{32.2}{2.2}} = 23.1$

Area of Orifice, $A_o = 0.0218$ sq ft

Then: Coefficient of Velocity, $C_v = \frac{V}{V_i} = \frac{23.1}{24.1} = \underline{0.96}$

Ideal Flow, $Q_i = A_o\sqrt{2gH} = A_oV_i = .0218 \times 24.1 = 0.525$ cfs

Actual Flow, $Q = \frac{18.9 \text{ cfm}}{60} = 0.315$ cfs

Coefficient of Discharge, $C_d = \frac{\text{Actual Flow}}{\text{Ideal Flow}} = \frac{.315}{.525} = \underline{0.600}$

Coefficient of Contraction, $C_c = \frac{A_j}{A_o} = \frac{C_d}{C_c} = \frac{0.600}{0.960} = \underline{0.625}$

Area of jet, $A_j = C_C A_O = 0.625 \times 0.0218 = 0.0136$ sq ft

Diameter of jet, $D_j = \sqrt{\frac{.0136 \times 4}{\pi}} = 0.132$ ft Or, $\underline{1.58 \text{ inches}}$

10. CORRECT ANSWER: 2.36 cfs; Increase the flow over the weir.

This is a suppressed weir.
$Z = 2$ ft., $H - .5$ ft, $b = 2$ ft, $A_C = 2 \times 2.5 = 5$ sq ft

12 (#1)

$$Q = 3.33\, bH^{3/2}\left[1+0.26\left(\frac{bH}{A_c}\right)^2\right]$$

$$= 3.33 \times 2 \times .5^{5/2}\left[1+0.26\left(\frac{2 \times .5}{5}\right)^2\right] = \underline{2.36\text{ cfs}}$$

The velocity of approach tends to increase the flow over the weir.

11. **CORRECT ANSWER: 70.5 cfs**

   Suppressed weir.

   $$Q = 3.33 \times 3 \times 3.5^{\frac{3}{2}}\left[1+0.26\left(\frac{3 \times 3.5}{19.5}\right)^2\right] = \underline{70.5\text{ cfs}}$$

12. **CORRECT ANSWER: The bulkhead sections will be overtopped.**

   The discharge of an overflow spillway is given by Weir Equation: $Q = CbH^{3/2}$
   Assume the reservoir level is at the top of the bulkhead sections:

   Then: $Q = 3.85 \times 80 \times 8^{3/2} = 6970$ cfs
   Since the flow is 7600 cfs, then the bulkhead sections will be overtopped.

13. **CORRECT ANSWER: 1.6 cfs**

   The formula for flow of water in cfs over a triangular weir is:

   $$Q = \frac{8}{15} C \tan\frac{\theta}{2} \sqrt{2g}\, H^{5/2}$$

   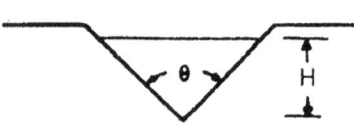

   Where: H = head on crest of weir in feet
   θ = vertex angle of notch
   C = coefficient with value between .58 and .60
   C = .58 for H less than 1 ft and .60 for heads greater than 1 foot

   For θ equal to 90°, the formula becomes: $Q = 4.28\, CH^{5/2}$

   Since θ equals 90° and H equals .833 ft, assume that C equals .59

   Then: $Q = 4.28 \times .59 \times \sqrt{.833^5} = \underline{1.6\text{ cfs}}$

14. **CORRECT ANSWER: 1.25 cfs**

   Solution: $Q = 4.28 \times .6 \times \sqrt{.75^5} = \underline{1.25\text{ cfs}}$

15. **CORRECT ANSWER: 0.425 cfs; 29.7 psi**

13 (#1)

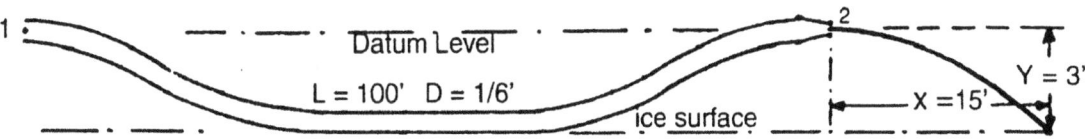

Since there is no contraction, then, $C_d = C_v = .90$

Actual velocity of nozzle jet, $V_n = X\sqrt{\dfrac{g}{2y}} = 15\sqrt{\dfrac{32.2}{2 \times 3}} = 34.7$ fps

Actual Flow, $Q = A_n V_n = .0123 \times 34.7 = \underline{0.425 \text{ cfs}}$

Bernoulli's Equation between points 1 and 2:

$$\dfrac{V_1^2}{2g} + \dfrac{p_1}{w} + z_1 - H_L = \dfrac{V_2^2}{2g} + \dfrac{p_2}{2} + z_2$$

Total Head Loss, $H_L = H_f + H_n$

Reynolds Number, $N_R = \dfrac{DV}{\nu} = \dfrac{1/6 \times 19.5}{1.2 \times 10^{-5}} = 2.7 \times 10^5$

Assume the rubber is a Smooth Pipe on the Moody Chart.

When $N_R = 2.7 \times 10^5$ then, $f = .0145$ it

Then: Friction Head Loss, $H_f = f \times \dfrac{L}{D} \times \dfrac{V_1^2}{2g} = .0145 \times \dfrac{100}{1/6} \times \dfrac{19.5^2}{64.4} = 51.3$ ft

Nozzle Head Loss, $H_n = (\dfrac{1}{C_v^2} - 1) \dfrac{V_n^2}{2} = (\dfrac{1}{.9^2} - 1)\dfrac{34.7^2}{64.4} = 4.4$ ft

Substituting in Bernoulli's Equation:

$$\dfrac{19.5^2}{64.4} + \dfrac{p_1 \times 144}{62.4} + 0 - (51.3 + 4.4)\dfrac{34.7^2}{64.4} + 0 + 0$$

Solving for pressure, p_1, at the valve upstream = $\underline{29.7 \text{ psi}}$

16. CORRECT ANSWER: 1590

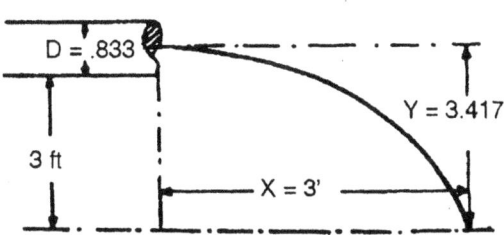

There is no Coefficient of Contraction.

Actual Velocity, $V = 3\sqrt{\dfrac{32.2}{2 \times 3.417}} = 6.5$ fps

Area of pipe, $A = .545$ sq ft

Actual Flow, $Q = AV = .545 \times 6.5 = 3.54$ cfs

GPM = $3.54 \times 7.5 \times 60 = \underline{1590}$

17. CORRECT ANSWER: 4130 gpm

From Bernoulli's Equation between points 1 and 2 and that Q = AV, it can be proved that, for a venturi meter:

Quantity Flow, $Q = c_d A_1 A_2 \sqrt{\dfrac{2g\left(\dfrac{p_1-p_2}{w}\right)}{A_1^2 - A_2^2}}$ in cu ft per sec

Where: C_d = Discharge Coefficient or Meter Constant = 0.95
A_1 = Area of main pipe = for 20" dia. = 2.18 sq ft
A_2 = Area of meter throat = for 8" dia. = 0.349 sq ft

$\dfrac{p_1 - p_2}{w}$ = difference in pressure head in feet of the fluid flowing in meter

w = weight per cu ft of fluid flowing
p = pressure in psf

Given: $P_1 - P_2 = 5 \times 144 = 720$ psf

Then: $Q = .95 \times 2.18 \times .349 \sqrt{\dfrac{64.4 \times \dfrac{720}{62.4}}{2.18^2 - .349^2}} = 9.2$ cfs or 4130 gpm

18. CORRECT ANSWER: 26.4 feet

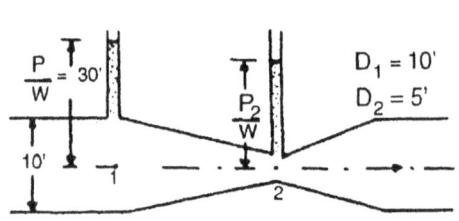

Areas: A_1 = 78.54 sq ft
A_2 = 19.64 sq ft

$Q = C_d A_1 A_2 \times \sqrt{\dfrac{2g\left(\dfrac{p_1}{w} - \dfrac{p_2}{w}\right)}{A_1^2 - A_2^2}}$

Then: $300 = 0.98 \times 78.54 \times 19.64 \times \sqrt{\dfrac{2 \times 32.2 \times \left(30 - \dfrac{p_2}{w}\right)}{(78.54)^2 - (19.64)^2}}$

Solving the above equation: $\dfrac{p_2}{w}$ = 26.4 feet

19. CORRECT ANSWER: 1010 gpm

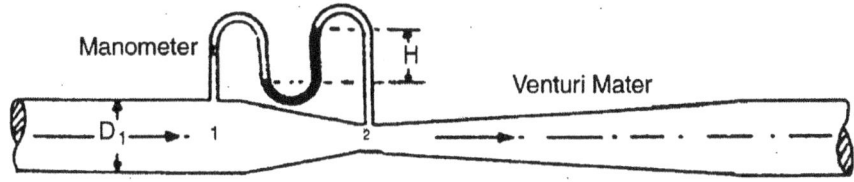

It can be proved for a differential gage that:

$\dfrac{p_1-p_2}{w} = H\left(\dfrac{w_g}{w}-1\right)$ = difference in pressure head in feet of the fluid flowing through the

Where: H = gage reading in feet, p_1 and p_2 are in psf
w_g = weight per cu ft of the gage fluid, or specific gravity
w = weight per cu ft of the fluid flowing in pipe, or sp. gr.

Then: $\dfrac{p_1-p_2}{w} = \dfrac{8}{12}\left(\dfrac{13.6}{.95}-1\right) = 8.9$ feet of oil

And: $Q = .98 \times .196 \times .087 \sqrt{\dfrac{64.4 \times 8.9}{.196^2 - .087^2}} = 2.26$ cfs or <u>1010 gpm</u>

20. CORRECT ANSWER: 1.3'; 11 cfs

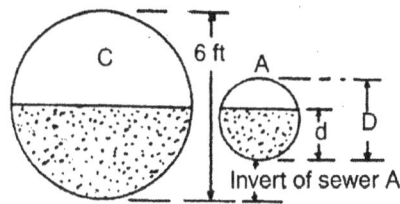

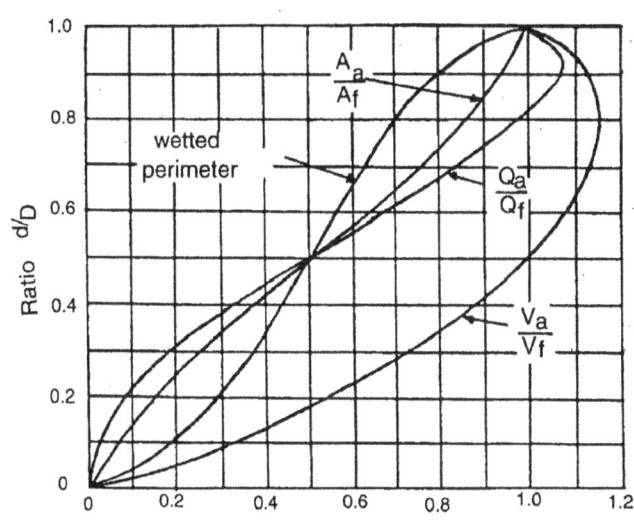

d = depth of flow in ft
D = internal diameter
Q = flow in cfs
A = area of flow in sq ft
V = velocity of flow in fps
Subscript a is actual flow
Subscript f is full flow

The invert of a pipe is the elevation of the lowest point of its interior surface.

$\dfrac{Q_a}{Q_f}, \dfrac{V_a}{V_f}, \dfrac{A_a}{A_f},$ and $\dfrac{WP_a}{WP_f}$

For circular pipe flowing full or half full:

16 (#1)

Hydraulic Radius, $R = \dfrac{D}{4}$

The level of flow in sewer A must be at the same level as in sewer C in order that no sewage will back up in sewer A above the level of its maximum flow.

Max. flow in sewer A, $Q_a = A_a \times \dfrac{1.486}{0.013} \times \left(\dfrac{A_a}{WP_a}\right)^{2/3} \times .002^{\frac{1}{2}} = 15$ cfs (given)

Both the area of flow, A_a, and the wetted perimeter, WP_a, are unknown. To find the depth of flow, d, the problem must be solved by trial and error unless suitable charts are available. This type of problem is often encountered in hydraulic engineering particularly in the case of circular sewers flowing partly full as in this case. To facilitate solution of this type of problem, a chart as shown is generally available which shows:

$$\dfrac{\text{depth of flow (d)}}{\text{Diameter of sewer (D)}} \text{ vs } \dfrac{\text{ActualFlow}(Q_a)}{\text{FullFlow}(Q_f)} \quad \text{Or,} \quad \dfrac{d}{D} \text{ vs } \dfrac{Q_a}{Q_f}$$

For sewer $A: Q_f = (\pi \times 1.25^2) \times \dfrac{1.486}{0.013} \times \left(\dfrac{2.5}{4}\right)^{2/3} \times .002^{\frac{1}{2}} = 18.4$ cfs

Then: $\dfrac{Q_a}{Q_f} = \dfrac{15}{18.4} = 0.815$ Then, from Chart: $\dfrac{d}{D} = 0.68$ (D = 2.5ft)

And, d = 0.68 x 2.5 = 1.7 ft And, Invert of A from invert of C = 3 - 1.7 = <u>1.3'</u>

For C flowing half-full: $Q_c = \dfrac{(\pi \times 3^2)}{2} \times \dfrac{1.486}{0.013} \times \left(\dfrac{6}{4}\right)^{2/3} \times .0006^{\frac{1}{2}} = 26$ cfs

Flow in sewer B: $Q_B = Q_C - Q_A = 26 - 15 = \underline{11\ cfs}$

21. CORRECT ANSWER: 16.2 cfs

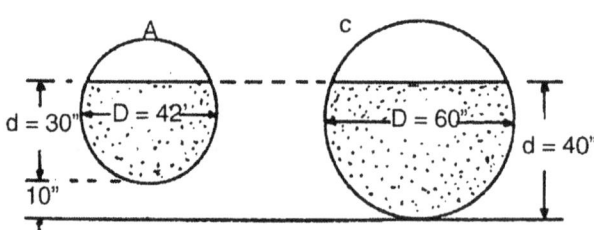

$A_A = \dfrac{\pi \times 3.5^2}{4} = 9.62$ sq ft, $A_C = \dfrac{\pi \times 5^2}{4} = 19.6$ sq ft

R for full or half-full flow = $\dfrac{D}{4}$

n = .013

For sewer A: $\dfrac{d}{D} = \dfrac{30}{42} = 0.715$ From Chart, $\dfrac{Q_a}{Q_f} = 0.86$

$Q_f = 9.62 \times \dfrac{1.486}{0.013} \times \left(\dfrac{3.5}{4}\right)^{2/3} \times .006^{\frac{1}{2}} = 63.7$ cfs

17 (#1)

Actual Flow, $Q_A = 38.9 \times 0.86 = 33.5$ cfs

For sewer C: $\dfrac{d}{D} = \dfrac{40}{60} = 0.667$ From Chart, $\dfrac{Q_a}{Q_f} = 0.78$

$Q_f = 19.6 \times \dfrac{1.486}{0.013} \times (\dfrac{6}{4})^{2/3} \times .0006^{1/2} = 63.7$ cfs

Actual Flow, $Q_c = 63.7 \times 0.78 = 48.7$ cfs
Flow in sewer B: $Q_B = Q_C - Q_A = 49.7 - 33.5 = \underline{16.2 \text{ cfs}}$

22. CORRECT ANSWER: 20,150 cfs

This problem may be solved by using a weighted average for the value of Kutter's roughness factor, n, for the two types of surface and consider a single area of channel flow, or it may be solved by considering three sections of flow.

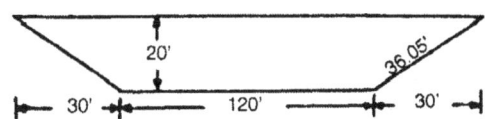

Paved: Use n = .013 of ordinary concrete
Gravel: Use n = .021 of firm gravel

Weighted average value of n:

$n_o = \dfrac{120 \times .021 + 72.1 \times .013}{120 + 72.1} = .018$

Wetted Perimeter, $WP = 120 + 2 \times \sqrt{20^2 + 30^2} = 120 + 72.1 = 192.1$ ft
Area of Flow, $A = 120 \times 20 + 30 \times 20 = 3000$ sq ft

$R = \dfrac{A}{WP} = \dfrac{3000}{192.1} = 15.6'$

$Q = A \times \dfrac{1.486}{n} \times R^{2/3} \times S^{1/2} = 3000 \times \dfrac{1.486}{.018} \times (15.6)^{2/3} \times (\dfrac{.90}{5280})^{1/2} = \underline{20,150 \text{ cfs}}$

23. CORRECT ANSWER: 6.6 ft

Area of 8" pipe, $A_p = 0.349$ sq ft, $Q = A_p V_1 = .349 \times 12 = 4.19$ cfs

Average velocity in slit, $V_{av} = \dfrac{12 + (12 + L)}{2} = 12 + 0.5L$

Area of slit, $A_s = \dfrac{.5}{12} \times L = 0.0417L$ sq ft

Flow through the slit, $Q = A_s V_{av}$ Or, $4.19 = (0.417L) \times (12 + 0.5L)$

From above equation: $L^2 + 24 - 200 = 0$ And, $L = \underline{6.6 \text{ ft}}$

24. CORRECT ANSWER: 5.22 cfs; 28 ft

The equation used to calculate the flow through a venturi meter may be used to calculate the flow through a nozzle discharging into the atmosphere.

18 (#1)

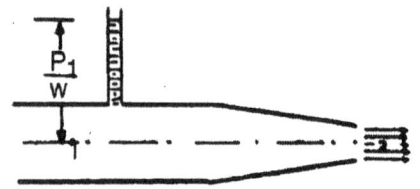

$$\frac{p_1-p_2}{w} = \frac{25 \times 144 - 0}{62.4} = 57.7 \text{ ft water}$$

$A_1 = .349$ sq ft, $A_2 = .087$ sq ft

$$Q = .95 \times .349 \times .087 \sqrt{\frac{64.4 \times 57.7}{.349^2 - .087^2}} = 5.22 \text{ cfs}$$

$$V = \frac{Q}{A_2} = \frac{5.22}{.087} = 60 \text{ fps}$$

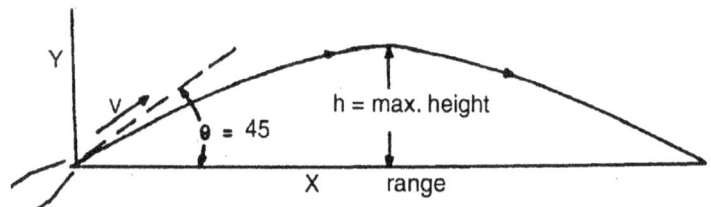

Horizontal displacement, $X = V\cos\theta \times t$ (Equation 1)

Vertical displacement, $Y = V\sin\theta \times t - \frac{1}{2}gt^2$ (Equation 2)

When $Y = 0$ (end of range), $t = \frac{2V\sin\theta}{g}$ (time of flight) (Equation 3)

For Max. height, any angle θ: $t = \frac{1}{2}(\frac{2V\sin\theta}{g}) = \frac{V\sin\theta}{g}$

When $\theta = 45°$: Substitute value of t in Equation 2.

$$Y = h = V^2\sin^2\theta - \frac{1}{2}g(\frac{V\sin\theta}{g})^2 = \frac{V^2\sin^2\theta}{2g} = \frac{60^2 \times .707^2}{64.4} = 28 \text{ ft}$$

When $\theta = 90°$, $\sin\theta = 1$ Then, Max. Height $h = \frac{V^2}{2g}$

The range R is obtained by substituting the value of t from Equation 3 in Equation 1:

Range, $R = \frac{V^2\sin 2\theta}{g}$ Maximum range When $\theta = 45°$

The above Equations may also be used in problems of firing projectiles.

25. CORRECT ANSWER: 755 cfs

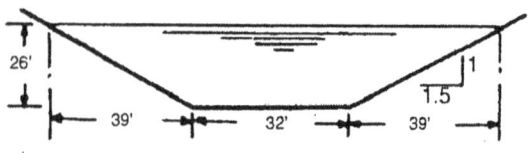 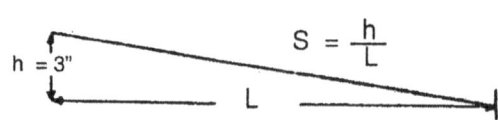

Hydraulic Radius, $R = \frac{A}{WP} = \frac{(32 \times 26) + (26 \times 39)}{32 + (2 \times \sqrt{39^2 + 26^2})} = \frac{1846}{126} = 14.65 \text{ ft}$

Slope of water surface, $S = \dfrac{h}{L} = \dfrac{\frac{1}{4} \text{ foot}}{\text{mile}} = \dfrac{0.25}{5280} = 0.0000474$

Roughness factor for concrete lining, n = .015

Then: $Q = AV = 1846 \times \dfrac{1.486}{0.015} \times \sqrt[3]{14.65^2} \times \sqrt{0000474} = 755$ cfs

26. CORRECT ANSWER: 3.12 ft

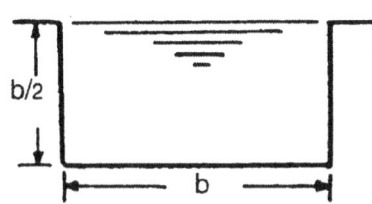

$Q = 50$ cfs, $V = \dfrac{Q}{A} = \dfrac{50}{b^2/2} = \dfrac{100}{b^2}$

$R = \dfrac{A}{WP} = \dfrac{b^2/2}{2b} = \dfrac{b}{4}$ Slope, $S = \dfrac{30}{2000} = 0.15$

$n = .015$

$\dfrac{100}{b^2} = \dfrac{1.486}{.015} \times \left(\dfrac{b}{4}\right)^{2/3} \times .015^{1/2}$

Then: $b^8 = 8950$ And, b = 3.12 ft

27. CORRECT ANSWER: .215 ft

$S = \dfrac{h}{L}$ $V = \dfrac{120}{40} = 3$ fps, $R = \dfrac{40}{18} = 2.22$ ft, $n = .013$

By Manning Formula: $3 = \dfrac{1.486}{.013} \times 2.22^{2/3} \times \left(\dfrac{h}{900}\right)^{1/2}$

And, h = .215 ft

28. CORRECT ANSWER: .55 ft

For concrete lining, $n = .015$, $R = \dfrac{R}{WP} = \dfrac{300}{48.3} = 6.21$ ft

Then: $050 = 300 \times \dfrac{1.486}{n} \times 6.21^{2/3} \times S^{1/2}$ And, $S = .0001045$

h = .55 ft

29. CORRECT ANSWER: 5000 cfs

(Depth of water = 15 feet)

30. CORRECT ANSWER: 74,340 cfs

20 (#1)

The procedure in this type of channel flow problem is to divide the flow area into separate sections and

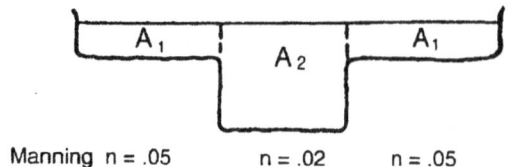

Manning n = .05   n = .02   n = .05

then solve for the flow in each section by Manning's Formula.
A_1 = 750 sq ft, A_2 = 2500 sq ft, R_1 = 4.69 ft, R_2 = 15 ft
V_1 = 5.1 fps, V_2 = 27.8 fps, Q_1 = 3820 cfs, Q_2 = 66,700 cfs
Total Flow, $Q = 2Q_1 + Q_2$ = 2x3820 + 66,700 = <u>74,340 cfs</u>

31. CORRECT ANSWER: 74,200 cfs

n = .04
Q = 74,200 cfs

32. CORRECT ANSWER: 4.55 fps; 7.14 cfs; 14.3 cfs

A combined sewer is one which conveys domestic and industrial sewage as well as storm water and must be designed to handle a peak flow.

n = .013 S = .004, A_1(half-full) = 1.57 sq ft,

$$R = \frac{D}{4} = \frac{2}{4} = 0.5$$

Velocity of Flow, $V_1 = \frac{1.486}{.015} \times 0.5^{2/3} \times .004^{1/2}$ = <u>4.55 fps</u>
Quantity of Flow, $Q_1 = AV$ = 1.57 x 4.55 = <u>7.14 cfs</u>
R_2 = same, S = same, V_2 = same, $A_2 = 2A_1$ = 3.14 sq ft
Then: Velocity, V_2 = 4.55 fps, And, Q_2 = 2x7.14 = <u>14.3 cfs</u>

33. CORRECT ANSWER: 14.3 cfs

34. CORRECT ANSWER: 2.76 in; 0.528 in

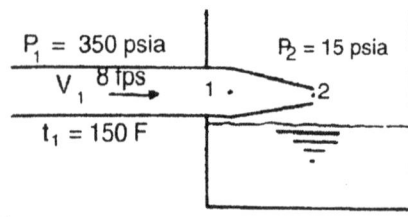

Assume nozzle coefficient, $C_v = 0.95$
At 150° F, w = 61.2 lb/cu ft

Flow, $Q = \frac{150 \text{ gpm}}{7.5 \times 60} = 0.333$ cfs

Nozzle loss, $H_L = (\frac{1}{C_v^2} - 1) \times \frac{V_2^2}{2g}$

21 (#1)

At (1): Area, $A_1 = \dfrac{Q}{V_1} = \dfrac{0.333}{8} = 0.0416$ sq ft

$D_1 = \sqrt{\dfrac{.0416 \times 4}{\pi}} = 2.76$ in

Bernoulli's Equation: $\dfrac{V_1^2}{2g} + \dfrac{P_1}{w} + Z_1 - H_L = \dfrac{V_2^2}{2g} + \dfrac{P_2}{w} + Z_2$

$H_L = \dfrac{V_1^2 - V_2^2}{2g} + \dfrac{P_1 - P_2}{w} = (\dfrac{1}{C_v^2} - 1) \times \dfrac{V_2^2}{2g}$

Then: $(\dfrac{1}{0.95^2} - 1) \times \dfrac{V_2^2}{64.4} = \dfrac{8^2 - V_2^2}{64.4} + \dfrac{350-15}{61.2}$ And, $V_2 = 219$ fps

$A_2 = \dfrac{Q}{V_2} = \dfrac{0.333}{219} = 0.00152$ sq ft, $D_2 = \sqrt{\dfrac{.00152 \times 4}{\pi}} = 0.528$ in

35. CORRECT ANSWER: 12,000 ft

Unit deformation, $e = \dfrac{f}{E} = \dfrac{50}{200,000} = .00025$ inch/inch

Total deformation, $a = el = 3' \times 12 = 36$ inches (given)

Then: $l = \dfrac{a}{e} = \dfrac{36}{.00025} = 144,000$ inches

Distance to obstruction, $L = \dfrac{144,000}{12} = 12,000$ ft

36. CORRECT ANSWER: 57.7 psia

For vertical motion of a fluid, the pressure in psf at any point in the liquid is:
+ = acceleration up.
− = acceleration down

$p = wh \times (1 \pm \dfrac{a}{g})$

for mercury, w = 13.6 62.4 = 849 lb/cu ft

Total pressure, $p = 12 + (849 \times \dfrac{9}{12})(1 - \dfrac{300}{32.2}) \times \dfrac{1}{144} = 57.7$ psia

37. CORRECT ANSWER: .00885 lb-sec/ft$_2$

22 (#1)

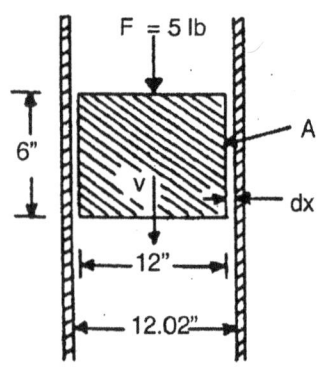

Absolute or (dynamic) viscosity, y = lb-sec/ft²

$$\frac{F}{A} = \mu \times \frac{dv}{dx}$$

Area, $A = \dfrac{\pi \times D_m \times \text{depth}}{144} = \dfrac{\pi \times 12.01 \times 6}{144} = 1.57$ sq ft

For the small space between the cylinder and the tube, the velocity gradient may be assumed to be a straight line.

$$\frac{dv}{dx} = \frac{0.6 \text{ ft/sec}}{0.2/12 \text{ ft}} = \frac{0.6 \text{ ft/sec}}{.00167 \text{ ft}}$$

$$\mu = \frac{5 \text{lb} \times .00167 \text{ ft}}{1.57 \text{ ft}^2 \times .6 \text{ ft/sec}} = .00885 \text{ lb-sec/ft}^2$$

38. CORRECT ANSWER: D

39. CORRECT ANSWER: C

40. CORRECT ANSWER: E

41. CORRECT ANSWER: A

BASIC FUNDAMENTALS OF WATER POLLUTION

TABLE OF CONTENTS

	Page
COLLECTING AND TREATING WASTES	1
Primary Treatment	2
Secondary Treatment	3
Lagoons and Septic Tanks	4
THE NEED FOR FURTHER TREATMENT OF WASTES	4
The Types of Pollutants	5
Oxygen-demanding Wastes	5
Disease-causing Agents	5
Plant Nutrients	5
Synthetic Organic Chemicals	5
Inorganic Chemicals and Mineral Substances	5
Sediments	6
Radioactive Substances	6
Heat	6
ADVANCED METHODS OF TREATING WASTES	6
Coagulation-Sedimentation	7
Adsorption	7
Electrodialysis	8
The Blending of Treated Water	8
NEW CHALLENGES FOR WASTE TREATMENT	9
Chemical Oxidation	9
Polymers and Pollution	10
THE PROBLEM OF WASTE DISPOSAL	10

BASIC FUNDAMENTALS OF WATER POLLUTION

COLLECTING AND TREATING WASTES

The most common form of pollution control in the United States consists of a system of sewers and waste treatment plants. The sewers collect the waste water from homes, businesses, and many industries and deliver it to the plants for treatment to make it fit for discharge into streams or for reuse.

There are two kinds of sewer systems — combined and separate. Combined sewers carry away both water polluted by human use and water polluted as it drains off homes, streets, or land during a storm.

In a separated system, one system of sewers, usually called sanitary, carries only sewage. Another system of storm sewers takes care of the large volumes of water from rain or melting snow.

Each home has a sewer or pipe which connects to the common or lateral sewer beneath a nearby street. Lateral sewers connect with larger sewers called trunk or main sewers. In a combined sewer system, these trunk or main sewers discharge into a larger sewer called an interceptor. The interceptor is designed to carry several times the dry-weather flow of the system feeding into it.

During dry weather when the sewers are handling only the normal amount of waste water, all of it is carried to the waste treatment plant. During a storm when the amount of water in the sewer system is much greater, part of the water, including varying amounts of raw sewage, is allowed to bypass directly into the receiving streams. The rest of the wastes are sent to the treatment plant. If part of the increased load of water were not diverted, the waste treatment plant would be overloaded and the purifying processes would not function properly. (A research, development, and demonstration program is being conducted to solve this urban runoff pollution problem. The aim is to develop technology that will control and/or treat combined sewer overflows, storm water discharges, and general washoff of rainwater polluted by dirt or other contaminants on the land.)

Interceptor sewers are also used in sanitary sewer systems as collectors of flow from main sewers and trunks, but do not normally include provisions for bypassing.

A waste treatment plant's basic function is to speed up the natural processes by which water purifies itself. In many cases, nature's treatment process in streams and lakes was adequate before our population and industry grew to their present size.

When the sewage of previous years was dumped into waterways, the natural process of purification began. First, the sheer volume of clean water in the stream diluted the small amount of wastes. Bacteria and other small organisms in the water consumed the sewage or other organic matter, turning it into new bacterial cells, carbon dioxide, and other products.

But the bacteria normally present in water must have oxygen to do their part in breaking down the sewage. Water acquires this all important oxygen by absorbing it from the air and from plants that grow in the water itself. These plants use sunlight to turn the carbon dioxide present in water into oxygen.

The life and death of any body of water depend mainly upon its ability to maintain a certain amount of dissolved oxygen. This dissolved oxygen — or DO — is what fish breathe. Without it, they suffocate. If only a small amount of sewage is dumped into a stream, fish are not affected, and the bacteria can do their work and the stream can quickly restore its oxygen loss from the atmosphere and from plants. Trouble begins when the sewage load is excessive. The sewage will decay and the water will begin to give off odors. If carried to the extreme, the water could lose all of its oxygen, resulting in the death of fish and beneficial plant life.

Since dissolved oxygen is the key element in the life of water, the demands on it are used as a measure in telling how well a sewage treatment plant is working. This measuring device is called biochemical oxygen demand, or BOD. If the effluent or the end-product from a treatment plant has a high content of organic pollutants, the effluent will have a high BOD. In other words, it will demand more oxygen from the water to break down the sewage and consequently will leave the water with less oxygen (and also dirtier).

With the growth of the nation, the problems of pollution have become more complex. The increased amounts of wastes and the larger demands for water have reduced the capacity of running water to purify itself. Consequently, cities and industry have had to begin thinking about removing as much as possible of the oxygen-demanding pollutants from their sewage.

Adequate treatment of wastes along with providing a sufficient supply of clean water has become a major concern.

Primary Treatment

At present, there are two basic ways of treating wastes. They are called primary and secondary. In primary treatment, solids are allowed to settle and are removed from the water Secondary treatment, a further step in purifying waste water, uses biological processes.

As sewage enters a plant for primary treatment, it flows through a screen. The screen removes large floating objects such as rags and sticks that may clog pumps and small pipes. The screens vary from coarse to fine — from those with parallel steel or iron bars with openings of about half an inch or more to screens with much smaller openings.

Screens are generally placed in a chamber or channel in an inclined position to the flow of the sewage to make cleaning easier. The debris caught on the upstream surface of the screen can be raked off manually or mechanically.

Some plants use a device known as a comminutor which combines the functions of a screen and a grinder. These devices catch and then cut or shred the heavy solid material. In the process, the pulverized matter remains in the sewage flow to be removed later in a settling tank.

After the sewage has been screened, it passes into what is called a grit chamber where sand, grit, cinders, and small stones are allowed to settle to the bottom. A grit chamber is highly important for cities with combined sewer systems because it will remove the grit or gravel that washes off streets or land during a storm and ends up at treatment plants.

The unwanted grit or gravel from this process is usually disposed of by filling land near a treatment plant.

In some plants, another screen is placed after the grit chamber to remove any further material that might damage equipment or interfere with later processes.

With the screening completed and the grit removed, the sewage still contains dissolved organic and inorganic matter along with suspended solids. The latter consist of minute particles of matter that can be removed from the sewage by treatment in a sedimentation tank. When the speed of the flow of sewage through one of these tanks is reduced, the suspended solids will gradually sink to the bottom. This mass of solids is called raw sludge.

Various methods have been devised for removing sludge from the tanks.

In older plants, sludge removal was done by hand. After a tank had been in service for several days or weeks, the sewage flow was diverted to another tank. The sludge in the bottom of the out-of-service tank was pushed or flushed with water to a pit near the tank and then removed, usually by pumping, for further treatment or disposal.

Almost all plants built within the past 30 years have had a mechanical means for removing the sludge from sedimentation tanks. Some plants remove it continuously while others remove it at intervals.

To complete the primary treatment, the effluent from the sedimentation tank is chlorinated before being discharged into a stream or river. Chlorine gas is fed into the water to kill and reduce the number of disease-causing bacteria. Chlorination also helps to reduce objectionable odors.

Although 30 percent of the municipalities in the United States give only primary treatment to their sewage, this process by itself is considered entirely inadequate for most needs.

Today's cities and industry, faced with increased amounts of wastes and wastes that are more difficult to remove from water, have turned to secondary and even advanced waste treatment.

Secondary Treatment

Secondary treatment removes up to 90 percent of the organic matter in sewage by making use of the bacteria in it. The two principal types of secondary treatment are trickling filters and the activated-sludge process.

The trickling filter process or the activated-sludge process is used mostly today. After the effluent leaves the sedimentation tank in the primary stage of treatment, it flows or is pumped to a facility using one or the other of these processes. A trickling filter is simply a bed of stones from three to ten feet deep through which the sewage passes. Bacteria gather and multiply on these stones until they can consume most of the organic matter in the sewage. The cleaner water trickles out through pipes in the bottom of the filter for further treatment.

The sewage is applied to the bed of stones in two principal ways. One method consists of distributing the effluent intermittently through a network of pipes laid on or beneath the surface of the stones.

Attached to these pipes are smaller, vertical pipes which spray the sewage over the stones.

Another much-used method consists of a vertical pipe in the center of the filter connected to rotating horizontal pipes which spray the sewage continuously upon the stones.

The trend today is toward the use of the activated sludge process instead of trickling filters. This process speeds up the work of the bacteria by bringing air and sludge heavily laden with bacteria into close contact with the sewage.

After the sewage leaves the settling tank in primary treatment, it is pumped to an aeration tank where it is mixed with air and sludge loaded with bacteria and allowed to remain for several hours. During this time, the bacteria break down the organic matter.

From the aeration tank, the sewage, now called mixed liquor, flows to another sedimentation tank to remove the solids. Chlorination of the effluent completes the basic secondary treatment.

The sludge, now activated with additional millions of bacteria and other tiny organisms, can be used again by returning it to an aeration tank for mixing with new sewage and ample amounts of air.

The activated sludge process, like most other techniques, has advantages and limitations. The size of the units necessary for this treatment is small, thereby requiring less land space and the process is free of flies and odors. But it is more costly to operate than the filter, and the activated sludge process sometimes loses its effectiveness when faced with difficult industrial wastes.

An adequate supply of oxygen is necessary for the activated sludge process to be effective. Air is mixed with sewage and biologically active sludge in the aeration tanks by three different methods.

The first, mechanical aeration, is accomplished by drawing the sewage from the bottom of the tank and spraying it over the surface, thus causing the sewage to absorb large amounts of oxygen from the atmosphere.

In the second method, large amounts of air under pressure are piped down into the sewage and forced out through openings in the pipe. The third method is a combination of mechanical aeration and the force air method.

The final phase of the secondary treatment consists of the addition of chlorine, as the most common method of disinfection, to the effluent coming from the trickling filter or the activated sludge process. Chlorine is usually purchased in liquid form, converted to a gas, and injected into the effluent 15 to 30 minutes before the treated water is discharged into a watercourse. If done properly, Chlorination will kill more than 99 percent of the harmful bacteria in an effluent.

Lagoons and Septic Tanks

There are many well-populated areas in the United States that are not served by any sewer systems or waste treatment plants. Lagoons and septic tanks may act as less than satisfactory alternatives at such locations.

A septic tank is simply a tank buried in the ground to treat the sewage from an individual home. Waste water from the home flows into the tank where bacteria in the sewage may break down the organic matter and the cleaner water flows out of the tank into the ground through sub-surface drains. Periodically, the sludge or solid matter in the bottom of the tank must be removed and disposed of.

In a rural setting, with the right kind of soil and the proper location, the septic tank may be a reasonable and temporary means of disposing of strictly domestic wastes. Septic tanks should always be located so that none of the effluent can seep into sources used for drinking.

Lagoons, or, as they are sometimes called, stabilization or oxidation ponds, also have several advantages when used correctly.

They can give sewage primary and secondary treatment or they can be used to supplement other processes.

A lagoon is a scientifically constructed pond, usually three to five feet deep, in which sunlight, algae, and oxygen interact to restore water to a quality that is often equal to or better than effluent from secondary treatment. Changes in the weather may change the effectiveness of lagoons.

When used with other waste treatment processes, lagoons can be very effective. A good example of this is the Santee, California, water reclamation project. After conventional primary and secondary treatment by activated sludge, the town's waste water is kept in a lagoon for 30 days. Then the effluent, after chlorination, is pumped to land immediately above a series of lakes and allowed to trickle down through sandy soil into the lakes. The resulting water is of such good quality the residents of the area can swim, boat, and fish in the lake water.

THE NEED FOR FURTHER TREATMENT OF WASTES

In the past, pollution control was concerned primarily with problems caused by domestic and the simpler wastes of industry. Control was aimed principally towards protecting downstream public water supplies and stopping or preventing nuisance conditions.

Pollution problems were principally local in extent and their control a local matter.

This is no longer true. National growth and change have altered this picture. Progress in abating pollution has been outdistanced by population growth, the speed of industrial progress and technological developments, changing land practices, and many other factors.

The increased production of goods has greatly increased the amounts of common industrial wastes. New processes in manufacturing are producing new, complex wastes that sometimes defy present pollution control technology. The increased application of commercial fertilizers and the development and widespread use of a vast array of new pesticides are resulting in a host of new pollution problems from water draining off land.

The growth of the nuclear energy field and the use of radioactive materials foreshadow still another complicating and potentially serious water pollution situation.

Long stretches of both interstate and intrastate streams are subjected to pollution which ruins or reduces the use of the water for many purposes. Conventional biological waste treatment processes are hard-pressed to hold the pollution line, and for a growing number of our larger cities, these processes are no longer adequate.

Our growing population not only is packing our central cities but spreading out farther and farther into suburbia and exurbia. Across the country, new satellite communities are being born almost daily. The construction or extension of sewer lines has not matched either the growth rate or its movements. Sea water intrusion is a growing problem in coastal areas. It is usually caused by the excessive pumping of fresh water from the ground which lowers the water level, allowing salt water to flow into the ground water area.

The Types of Pollutants

Present-day problems that must be met by sewage treatment plants can be summed up in the eight types of pollutants affecting our waters.

The eight general categories are: common sewage and other oxygen-demanding wastes; disease-causing agents; plant nutrients; synthetic organic chemicals; inorganic chemicals and other mineral substances; sediment; radioactive substances; and heat.

Oxygen-demanding wastes — These are the traditional organic waste and ammonia contributed by domestic sewage and industrial wastes of plant and animal origin. Besides human sewage, such wastes result from food processing, paper mill production, tanning, and other manufacturing processes. These wastes are usually destroyed by bacteria if there is sufficient oxygen present in the water. Since fish and other aquatic life depend on oxygen for life, the oxygen-demanding wastes must be controlled, or the fish die.

Disease-causing agents — This category includes infectious organisms which are carried into surface and ground water by sewage from cities and institutions, and by certain kinds of industrial wastes, such as tanning and meat packing plants. Man or animals come in contact with these microbes either by drinking the water or through swimming, fishing, or other activities. Although modern disinfection techniques have greatly reduced the danger of this type of pollutant, the problem must be watched constantly.

Plant nutrients — These are the substances in the food chain of aquatic life, such as algae and water weeds, which support and stimulate their growth. Carbon, nitrogen, and phosphorus are the three chief nutrients present in natural water. Large amounts of these nutrients are produced by sewage, certain industrial wastes, and drainage from fertilized lands. Biological waste treatment processes do not remove the phosphorus and nitrogen to any substantial extent -- in fact, they convert the organic forms of these substances into mineral form, making them more usable by plant life. The problem starts when an excess of these nutrients over-stimulates the growth of water plants which cause unsightly conditions, interfere with treatment processes, and cause unpleasant and disagreeable tastes and odors in the water.

Synthetic organic chemicals — Included in this category are detergents and other household aids, all the new synthetic organic pesticides, synthetic industrial chemicals, and the wastes from their manufacture. Many of these substances are toxic to fish and aquatic life and possibly harmful to humans. They cause taste and odor problems and resist conventional waste treatment. Some are known to be highly poisonous at very low concentrations. What the long-term effects of small doses of toxic substances may be is not yet known.

Inorganic chemicals and mineral substances — A vast array of metal salts, acids, solid matter, and many other chemical compounds are included in this group. They reach our waters from mining and manufacturing processes, oil field operations, agricultural practices, and natural sources. Water used in irrigation picks up large amounts of minerals as it filters down through the soil on its way to the nearest stream. Acids of a wide variety are discharged as wastes by industry, but the largest single source of acid in our water comes from mining operations and mines that have been abandoned. Many of these types of chemicals are being created each year. They interfere with natural stream purification, destroy fish and other aquatic life, cause excessive hardness of water supplies, corrode expensive water treatment equipment, increase commercial and recreational boat maintenance costs, and boost the cost of waste treatment.

Sediments — These are the particles of soils, sands, and minerals washed from the land and paved areas of communities into the water. Construction projects are often large sediment producers. While not as insidious as some other types of pollution, sediments are a major problem because of the sheer magnitude of the amount reaching our waterways. Sediments fill stream channels and harbors, requiring expensive dredging, and they fill reservoirs, reducing their capacities and useful life. They erode power turbines and pumping equipment, and reduce fish and shellfish populations by blanketing fish nests and food supplies. More importantly, sediments reduce the amount of sunlight penetrating the water. The sunlight is required by green aquatic plants which produce the oxygen necessary to normal stream balance. Sediments greatly increase the treatment costs for municipal and industrial water supply and for sewage treatment where combined sewers are in use.

Radioactive substances — Radioactive pollution results from the mining and processing of radioactive ores; from the use of refined radioactive materials in power reactors and for industrial, medical, and research purposes; and from fallout following nuclear weapons testing. Increased use of these substances poses a potential public health problem. Since radiation accumulates in humans, control of this type of pollution must take into consideration total exposure in the human environment -- water, air, food, occupation, and medical treatment.

Heat — Heat reduces the capacity of water to absorb oxygen. Tremendous volumes of water are used by power plants and industry for cooling. Most of the water, with the added heat, is returned to streams, raising their temperatures. With less oxygen, the water is not as efficient in assimilating oxygen-consuming wastes and in supporting fish and aquatic life. Unchecked waste heat discharges can seriously alter the ecology of a lake, a stream, or even part of the sea.

Water in lakes or stored in impoundments can be greatly affected by heat. Summer temperatures heat up the surfaces, causing the water to form into layers, with the cooler water forming the deeper layers. Decomposing vegetative matter from natural and man-made pollutants deplete the oxygen from these cooler lower layers with harmful effects on the aquatic life. When the oxygen-deficient water is discharged from the lower gates of a dam, it may have serious effects on downstream fish life and reduce the ability of the stream to assimilate downstream pollution.

To complicate matters, most of our wastes are a mixture of the eight types of pollution, making the problems of treatment and control that much more difficult.

Municipal wastes usually contain oxygen-consuming pollutants, synthetic organic chemicals such as detergents, sediments, and other types of pollutants. The same is true of many industrial wastes which may contain, in addition, substantial amounts of heat from cooling processes. Water that drains off the land usually contains great amounts of organic matter in addition to sediment. Also, land drainage may contain radioactive substances and pollutants washed from the sky, vegetation, buildings, and streets during rainfall.

ADVANCED METHODS OF TREATING WASTES

These new problems of a modern society have placed additional burden upon our waste treatment systems. Today's pollutants are more difficult to remove from the water. And increased demands upon our water supply aggravate the problem. During the dry season, the flow of rivers decreases to such an extent that they have difficulty in assimilating the effluent from waste treatment plants.

In the future, these problems will be met through better and more complete methods of removing pollutants from water and better means for preventing some wastes from even reaching our streams in the first place.

The best immediate answer to these problems is the widespread application of existing waste treatment methods. Many cities that have only primary treatment need secondary treatment. Many other cities need enlarged or modernized primary and secondary systems.

But this is only a temporary solution. The discharge of oxygen-consuming wastes will increase despite the universal application of the most efficient waste treatment processes now available. And these are the simplest wastes to dispose of. Conventional treatment processes are already losing the battle against the modern-day, tougher wastes.

The increasing need to reuse water now calls for better and better waste treatment. Every use of water — whether in home, in the factory, or on the farm — results in some change in its quality.

To return water of more usable quality to receiving lakes and streams, new methods for removing pollutants are being developed. The advanced waste treatment techniques under investigation range from extensions of biological treatment capable of removing nitrogen and phosphorus nutrients to physical-chemical separation techniques such as adsorption, distillation, and reverse osmosis.

These new processes can achieve any degree of pollution control desired and, as waste effluents are purified to higher and higher degrees by such treatment, the point is reached where effluents become *too good to throw away.*

Such water can be deliberately and directly reused for agricultural, industrial, recreational, or even drinking water supplies. This complete water renovation will mean complete pollution control and, at the same time, more water for the nation.

Coagulation-Sedimentation

The application of advanced techniques for waste treatment, at least in the next several years, will most likely take up where primary and secondary treatment leave off. Ultimately, entirely new systems will no doubt replace the modern facilities of today.

The process known as coagulation-sedimentation may be used to increase the removal of solids from effluent after primary and secondary treatment. Besides removing essentially all of the settleable solids, this method can, with proper control and sufficient addition of chemicals, reduce the concentration of phosphate by over 95 percent.

In this process, alum, lime, or iron salts are added to effluent as it comes from the secondary treatment. The flow then passes through flocculation tanks where the chemicals cause the smaller particles to floc or bunch together into large masses.

The larger masses of particles or lumps will settle faster when the effluent reaches the next step — the sedimentation tank.

Although used for years in the treatment of industrial wastes and in water treatment, coagulation-sedimentation is classified as an advanced process because it is not usually applied to the treatment of municipal wastes. In many cases, the process is a necessary pre-treatment for some of the other advanced techniques.

Adsorption

Technology has also been developed to effect the removal of refractory organic materials. These materials are the stubborn organic matter which persists in water and resists normal biological treatment.

The effects of the organics are not completely understood, but taste and odor problems in water, tainting of fish flesh, foaming of water, and fish kills have been attributed to such materials.

Adsorption consists of passing the effluent through a bed of activated carbon granules which will remove more than 98 percent of the organics. To cut down the cost of the procedure, the carbon granules can be cleaned by heat and used again.

An alternative system utilizing powdered carbon is under study. Rather than pass the effluent through a bed of granules, the powdered carbon is put directly into the stream. The organics stick to the carbon, and then the carbon is removed from the effluent by using coagulating chemicals and allowing the coagulated carbon particles to settle in a tank.

The use of this finely ground carbon will improve the rate at which the refractory organics are removed. The potential widespread use of powdered carbon adsorption depends largely on the effectiveness of regenerating the carbon for use again.

Except for the salts added during the use of water, municipal waste water that has gone through the previous advanced processes will be restored to a chemical quality almost the same as before it was used.

When talking of salts in water, salt is not limited to the common kind that is used in the home for seasoning food. In waste treatment language, salts mean the many minerals dissolved by water as it passes through the air as rainfall, as it trickles through the soil and over rocks, and as it is used in the home and factory.

Electrodialysis

Electrodialysis is a rather complicated process by which electricity and membranes are used to remove salts from an effluent. A membrane is usually made of chemically treated plastic. The salts are forced out of the water by the action of an electric field. When a mineral salt is placed in water, it has a tendency to break down into ions. An ion is an atom or a small group of atoms having an electrical charge.

As an example, the two parts of common table salt are sodium and chlorine. When these two elements separate as salt dissolves in water, the sodium and chlorine particles are called ions. Sodium ions have a positive charge, while chlorine ions have a negative charge.

When the effluent passes through the electrodialysis cell, the positive sodium ions are attracted through a membrane to a pole or electrode that is negatively charged. The negatively charged chlorine ions are pulled out of the water through another membrane toward an electrode with a positive charge.

With the salts removed by the action of the two electrodes, the clean water flows out of the electrodialysis cell for reuse or discharge into a river or stream.

As a city uses its water, the amount of salts in the water increases by 300-400 milligrams per liter. Fortunately, electrodialysis can remove this buildup of salts.

In other words, this process returns the salt content of the water back to where it was or even better than when the city first received the water.

The Blending of Treated Water

Properly designed and applied, the methods that have been explained will be able to supply any quality of water for any reuse.

But none of these processes will stand alone. They must be used in a series or a parallel plan. In a series, all the sewage passes through all the processes, one after another, each process making a particular contribution toward improving the water. For example, the conventional primary treatment removes the material that will readily settle or float; the secondary biological step takes care of the decomposable impurities; coagulation-sedimentation, the third, step, eliminates the suspended solids; carbon adsorption removes the remaining dissolved organic matter; electrodialysis returns the level of the salts to what it was before the water was used; and, finally, chlorination provides the health safety barrier against disease carriers.

Basically, the same result can be achieved by separating the effluent into two streams. In this instance, all of the waste receives the primary and secondary treatment and then passes through the coagulation-sedimentation and adsorption processes which remove the organic matter. Half of the sewage is then treated by evaporation and adsorption to remove all impurities including the minerals. This effluent, when blended with the other half, can provide water with the desired level of minerals. After chlorination, the water can be reused.

Almost any degree of water quality can be achieved by varying the flow of the two streams. This technique reduces the treatment cost, since only a fraction of the flow requires treatment with the more expensive unit processes, such as distillation.

Distillation or evaporation basically consists of bringing the effluent to the boiling point. The steam or vapor produced is piped to another chamber where it is cooled, changing it back to a liquid. Most of the unwanted polluting impurities remain in the original chamber. However, some volatile substances may distill along with the water and carry along foreign materials that contribute objectionable taste.

As most people have discovered, distilled water has a flat, disagreeable taste caused by the absence of minerals and air. But by blending this pure water with water that still contains some minerals, a clean, better tasting water results. And, just as importantly, the more expensive distillation process is used on only part of the effluent, and the rest of the waste water is treated by the less costly procedures.

NEW CHALLENGES FOR WASTE TREATMENT

So far, the most readily available processes that will solve most current pollution problems have been covered. But the future holds many new challenges. Scientists are still looking for the ultimate system that will do the complete job of cleaning up water, simply and at a reasonable cost.

One such possible process under study is reverse osmosis. When liquids with different concentrations of mineral salts are separated by a membrane, molecules of pure water tend to pass by osmosis from the more concentrated to the less concentrated side until both liquids have the same mineral content.

Scientists are now exploring ways to take advantage of the natural phenomena of osmosis, but in reverse. When pressure is exerted on the side with the most minerals, this natural force reverses itself, causing the molecules of pure water to flow out of the compartment containing a high salt concentration.

This means that perfectly pure water is being taken out of the waste rather than taking pollutants out of water as is the traditional way. And this process takes clean water away from everything — bacteria, detergents, nitrates.

Tests have shown that the theory works well, resulting in water good enough to drink. Efforts are now under way to develop large membranes with long life. Also, the process and equipment need to be tested on a large scale.

Many other techniques to improve waste treatment are under development in laboratories and in the field.

For example, special microscopic organisms are being tested for removing nitrates from waste water by reducing the nitrates to elemental nitrogen.

Chemical Oxidation

Municipal waste waters contain many organic materials only partially removed by the conventional treatment methods. Oxidants such as ozone and chlorine have been used for many years to improve the taste and odor qualities or to disinfect municipal drinking water. They improve the quality of water by destroying or altering the structure of the chemicals in the water.

However, the concentration of the organic materials in drinking water supplies is much less than it is in the waste-bearing waters reaching treatment plants. Until recently, the cost of the oxidants has prevented the use of this process in the treating of wastes. Now improvements in the production and application of ozone and pure oxygen may reduce costs sufficiently to make their use practicable. When operated in conjunction with other processes, oxidation could become an effective weapon in eliminating wastes resistant to other processes.

Polymers and Pollution

In discussing the coagulation-sedimentation process, mention was made of the use of alum or lime to force suspended solids into larger masses. The clumping together helps speed up one of the key steps in waste treatment — the separation of solids and liquids.

During the past 25 years, the chemical industry has been working on synthetic organic chemicals, known as polyelectrolytes or polymers, to further improve the separation step.

Formerly, polymers have proved effective when used at a later stage of treatment -- the sludge disposal step. Sludge must be dewatered so that it can be more easily disposed of. By introducing polymers into the sludge, the physical and chemical bonds between the solids are tightened. When this happens, the water can be extracted more rapidly.

Wider use of polymers is now being investigated. By putting polymers into streams or rivers, it may be possible to capture silt at specified locations so that it can be removed in quantity.

If polymers are put into raw sewage, waste treatment plants may be able to combine a chemical process with the standard primary and secondary stages. And this method of removing solids can be applied immediately without lengthy and expensive addition of buildings or new facilities.

The chemicals also hold promise as a means of speeding the flow of waste waters through sewer systems, thus, in effect, increasing the capacity of existing systems.

THE PROBLEM OF WASTE DISPOSAL

No matter how good the treatment of wastes, there is always something left over. It may be the rags and sticks that were caught on the screens at the very beginning of the primary treatment. It could be brine or it could be sludge — that part of the sewage that settles to the bottom in sedimentation tanks. Whatever it is, there is always something that must be burned, buried, or disposed of in some manner.

It is a twofold problem. The sludge or other matter must be disposed of to complete a city's or industry's waste treatment. And it must be disposed of in a manner not to add to or upset the rest of the environment.

If it is burned, it must be done in a way not to add to the pollution of the atmosphere. This would only create an additional burden for our already overburdened air to cope with. And air pollutants by the action of rain and wind have a habit of returning to the water, complicating the waste treatment problem rather than helping it.

There are many methods and processes for dealing with the disposal problem, which is sometimes referred to as the problem of ultimate disposal. The most common method for disposing of sludge and other waste concentrates consists of digestion followed by filtration and incineration.

The digestion of sludge takes place in heated tanks where the material can decompose naturally and the odors can be controlled. As digested sludge consists of 90 to 95 percent water, the next step in disposal must be the removal of as much of the water as possible.

Water can be removed from sludge by use of a rotating filter drum and suction. As the drum rotates in the sludge, the water is pulled through the filter and the residues are peeled off for disposal. For more effective dewatering, the sludge can be first treated with a coagulant chemical such as lime or ferric chloride to produce larger solids before the sludge reaches the filter.

Drying beds which are usually made of layers of sand and gravel can be used to remove water from sludge. The sludge is spread over the bed and allowed to dry. After a week or two of drying, the residue will be reduced in volume and, consequently, will be easier to dispose.

Incineration consists of burning the dried sludge to reduce the residues to a safe, non-burnable ash. The ash can be disposed of by filling unused land or by dumping it well out into the ocean. Since most of the pollutants have been removed by the burning, the ash should cause very little change in the quality of the ocean waters.

A very promising new method of sludge disposal gets rid of the unwanted sludge and helps restore a ravaged countryside. In many areas of the country, tops of hills and mountains were sliced away to get at the coal beneath. This strip mining left ugly gashes and scars in otherwise beautiful valleys of many states. It would take nature many years to restore the denuded areas.

With the new disposal idea, digested sludge in semi-liquid form is piped to the spoiled areas. The slurry containing many nutrients from the wastes, is spread over the land to give nature a hand in returning grass, trees, and flowers to the barren hilltops.

Restoration of the countryside will also help in the control of acids that drain from mines into streams and rivers, endangering the fish and other aquatic life and adding to the difficulty in reusing the water. Acids are formed when pyrite containing iron and sulfur is exposed to the air.

Sludge or other waste concentrates are not always costly burdens. By drying and other processes, some cities have produced fertilizers that are sold to help pay for part of the cost of treating wastes. If not sold to the public, some municipalities use the soil enrichers on parks, road parkways, and other public areas.

Some industries have found they can reclaim certain chemicals during waste treatment and reuse them in manufacturing or refining processes. Other firms have developed saleable by-products from residues in waste treatment.

More studies are going on to find greater use for sludge to help solve the disposal problem and to help offset the cost of waste treatment.

www.ingramcontent.com/pod-product-compliance
Lightning Source LLC
Chambersburg PA
CBHW081830300426
44116CB00014B/2537